THE NUMBER ONE METHOD

LEARNING
ROYAL ARCH
CHAPTER
RITUAL

THE SIMPLE SYSTEMATIC AND SUCCESSFUL WAY TO MASTER THE WORK

Rick Smith

Author of the Best Selling 'Learning Masonic Ritual'

LEARNING ROYAL ARCH CHAPTER RITUAL

The Simple, Systematic and Successful Way to Master the Work

Rick Smith

www.learningmasonicritual.com
Published by Rick Smith
Copyright © Rick Smith 2013
All rights reserved.

Also available:

LEARNING MASONIC RITUAL
The Simple, Systematic and Successful Way to Master the Work

Table of Contents

Preface

How to Use This Book

Chapter 1 – Royal Arch Ritual Revealed!

Chapter 2 – The Challenges of Chapter Ritual

Chapter 3 – Making Your Plan

Chapter 4 – Learning and Memorising

Chapter 5 – Polishing & Refining

Chapter 6 – Chapter of Improvement

Chapter 7 – Rehearsal

Chapter 8 – The Day of the Meeting

Chapter 9 – Next Steps

Appendix - Recommended Timetable for Chapter Ceremonies

IMPORTANT NOTE; The Workings on which this book is based are predominately those of the Domatic and Aldersgate forms of Supreme Grand Chapter of England Ritual. Whilst these Learning Methods are suited to virtually any form of Masonic Ritual, the working examples may not be familiar to Royal Arch Masons from other Constitutions.

Preface

The Secret Weapons of Great Ritualists Revealed for Everyone to Use

If you are new to Royal Arch Masonry and facing this new and challenging Ritual for the first time, or alternately you have tried and struggled with Ritual in the past, it might be helpful to have a system to follow that will boost your chances of success. My previous book: "Learning Masonic Ritual – The Simple, Systematic and Successful Way to Master the Work" laid out an easy-to-follow process with a focus on structure and planning, to integrate learning and rehearsing into your everyday life.

In this book, these same methods are adapted and applied to Royal Arch Chapter Ritual, which can be even more demanding than Masonic Craft Ritual.

Many people struggle with Ritual because they simply don't have a reliable system for learning it.

How do great Ritualists make it look so easy? In this book, you will learn their techniques and processes, and how to apply them for yourself.

As you follow the step-by-step system in this book, you will learn;

- How to get offered the Work you want
- How to set up a Working Timetable so you peak at the right time

- The 3-Stage Plan that will keep you on-track
- Memorisation Tricks and Techniques
- How to find Rehearsal Time when there is none
- How to become a great Chapter Officer

This book also will show you how to avoid the big mistakes which people often make;

- They don't allow Enough Time
- They don't have a System, so they do it the hard way
- They fail to get the Hard Work done early, so they're always playing catch-up
- They don't utilise the Learning Aids that are littered throughout the Ritual
- They don't know how to Overcome Nerves and gain confidence

One of the most effective ways to advance your Masonic Enlightenment is to actively immerse yourself in becoming a competent Ritual performer in your Lodge or Chapter (hopefully both). There are many techniques you could employ, most of them very simple, and they are collected here for you to try. In places I have also drawn on my experience as a veteran communications professional and as a certified Clinical Hypnotherapist.

If you are starting out in the Chapter and looking for guidance in the Ritual System, or maybe you tried to learn Ritual but struggled with the performance aspects, this book is for you.

How to Use This Book

Learning Ritual is challenging. It isn't difficult in and of itself, but it takes time and patience to do it properly. As time goes by you find different methods that work better for you, and you eliminate the more time-consuming and less productive ways. You are evolving.

Given enough time you might eventually arrive at the perfect method, but it could take years of trial and error.

If you follow the System in this book, you will learn the most effective methods now, and you can immediately put them into practice.

Three Steps You Can Take

The first step in becoming a competent Ritualist is to commit to the process, to actually want to succeed.

The second step is to realise that, though it will look like a mountain ahead of you in the beginning, you have no reason to doubt your ability to climb it. Thousands have been there before you, and succeeded.

The third step is to take it head-on, using every tool and resource you can find, and master it. That's the way I did it, and over twenty years I was able to test and trial different techniques until I found a great system that works. I didn't invent this plan; it's the way that excellent Ritualists developed their skills and techniques, the ones they continue to use for many years, to 'make it look easy'.

A New Approach?

Time is the critical factor! Let's assume that you are motivated to succeed, but you also have a real life. If this is going to work for you, it cannot be disruptive. So, no long boring periods of study and no disruption to your daily routine.

You need a System.

Step-by-step you will learn a successful approach to memorising the Work and practising the delivery, ready for your big day in the Chapter. If you follow this systematic approach, trying all the elements until you find the personal combination that works for you, you will greatly improve your knowledge and capabilities for delivering strong Ritual performances in your Chapter.

The key Elements of this process are:

o Measuring the Work; understanding how much time you will need, and planning your timetable.
o Memorising the Ritual; Front-End Loading the process by diving in and quickly committing the key passages to memory.
o Polishing the Work; The right (and wrong) ways to really get to grips with your Ritual and eliminate all the obstacles to a great performance.
o Rehearsal, Preparation and Delivery; How it will be for you On The Day

You can use this book in various ways:

If you have read my previous book on Craft Ritual, you will already have been exposed to the learning methods, which are essentially repeated here. In this case, you may benefit from the specific sections on Chapter Ceremonies, which are different and arguably less familiar than those in the Craft.

If you are new to Ritual, you can read it from cover to cover, and get comfortable with the methodology. This way you can prepare the small adjustments that you'll need to make in your daily schedule, in advance of starting the learning itself. You will be able to understand the beginning, the middle, and the end, and you can pick out any areas which particularly apply to you. In this case, the book should be followed in Chapter sequence.

Alternately, you may just jump straight to the parts that you need, but in this case please make sure you read Chapter 3, which outlines the Three Stage System which you should be following.

Additional Resources

You can register for regular updates on www.learningmasonicritual.com and leave questions and comments in the Community section. Ask for help on specific Ritual, and someone is bound to have tips and tricks to add to your armoury.

There is also a Facebook Page, called Learning Masonic Ritual, which is a quick and easy way to interact with others who are using this system. Please have a look, and 'Like' the page if you would like to be include on the regular updates and conversations.

If you want to contact me directly, with any contributions, criticisms or suggestions, please feel free to e-mail me on rs@learningmasonicritual.com and I will endeavour to help wherever possible.

But most of all, if you find something in this book which helps you, and I truly hope you will, please leave an appropriate review on Amazon and give the book a star rating! Make your contribution to raising Ritual standards in our Lodges and Chapters, and make a positive contribution to the popularity and relevance of Freemasonry in the future.

Sincerely and Fraternally

Rick Smith

London, 2nd August 2013

Chapter 1
Royal Arch Ritual Revealed!

If you are new to the Royal Arch Chapter you may be feeling a little confused, especially if you have only recently completed the Three Degrees in Craft Masonry. Before you even have time to draw breath from your Raising Ceremony, you may have been persuaded that "in order to complete the Master Mason's Degree, you need to join Chapter".

Let's clear that up before we go any further.

The party line on the Holy Royal Arch of Jerusalem, to give it its full title, is currently that it is the Master Masons Degree completed. This is a relatively recent re-spin on the relationship between Craft and Chapter, because for many years Chapter was regarded in some quarters as the Fourth Degree. Although this specific relationship is no longer held to exist, it had a certain logic. Although all Master Masons (of four weeks and upward) are eligible to join the Chapter, only Past Masters of Craft Lodges were able to take one of the three Principal Offices in Chapter. Partly for this reason it was always viewed as a progression, and hence interpreted as a superior Degree.

This regulation is no longer in force. You can now progress right through the Chapter Offices, including the Office of First Principal, without having served as Master of a Craft Lodge.

We will explore the relationship between Craft and Chapter throughout this book, as it helps to put the whole Masonic experience into context. However, if you have read my previous book; "Learning Masonic Ritual – The Simple, Systematic and Successful Way to Master the Work", you will have understood that we are concerned mainly with the Ritual learning process, rather than any of the morality or greater meanings of Masonry. The deep meanings and lifelong lessons of Freemasonry are not meant to be learned from books; the reason you go to Lodge or Chapter is to assimilate the experience at first hand, and enjoyment of that is a major part of the mysteries and privileges associated with membership.

Chapter is Different

If you have attended you first Chapter meeting, you will already have experienced the obvious differences from the more familiar Craft Masonry environment. You will have observed that the Temple is laid out completely differently, although it still all focuses on the East. The Officers dress differently, although the basis is still black suits and white shirts. The most startling difference is in the ornaments, furniture and general paraphernalia. All those disparate items have significant meaning in the Ceremonies, even if it just looks like a pile of spare parts in the beginning, and if you choose to participate in the Ceremonies of the Chapter, you can soon learn all about them and what they represent.

In terms of Ritual, apart from the annual Installation of the new Principals there is only one Working Ceremony in Chapter, and that is the Exaltation for the admission of a new member. Because there is essentially nothing else for a Chapter to do apart from Exalt and progress new members, you can understand why recruitment is important. Like Craft Masonry, without new Candidates coming through there wouldn't be much work to do. However in the case of Chapter, there is only one 'Degree' so a new Candidate is really required for every meeting, otherwise we're back to the relatively mundane standard business of Charity Steward, Almoner, Treasurer Reports and so on.

As in the Craft, where the progression through the Offices and their associated Ritual is a preparation process for your Master's Year, in Chapter there is also a strong focus on getting you to the Principal's Chairs. If your Chapter is small, with less competition for offices, you could even be snapping at the heels of Third Principle within two or three years of joining. To do that you will probably have served at least one year as PS, and hopefully you will have participated in an Exaltation whilst you held that office. The PS work at Exaltation is a similar functional ceremony to JD at a Craft Initiation, but carries substantially more 'Lecture' style Ritual.

One subliminal difference between Chapter and Craft is this; by the time a Mason becomes eligible to join Chapter, he will have a decent understanding of the position and importance of Ritual in Freemasonry generally, which is not the case when first applying for membership of a Craft Lodge. So if your Chapter can develop a reputation for high-quality Ceremonial performances, word can get around and this helps a lot with the recruitment process.

Next, the Chapter Ritual is arguably more complex than Craft and not always easy to follow for non-combatants! Although not overtly religious, there are a lot of Scripture Readings in the Ceremonies, and this can be a bit dry and off-putting for some secular Companions.

So new Chapter members can sometimes lose interest quite quickly and stop attending. For this reason, it is a good idea to try to encourage the earliest participation in the Ritual and Proceedings of the Chapter, because once you start to get involved, you will discover a rich, challenging and beautiful set of Ceremonies which start to make logical sense once you're a part of them.

In the past few years, Supreme Grand Chapter has introduced 'Permitted Alternative Versions' (PAV) of the big ceremonies, which enable the work to be shared easily between more Companions. This has clear benefits. The complexity of the original Ceremonies (which are still permitted) is sometimes beyond the realistic capability of everyone to learn and perform, particularly since it is no longer stipulated that the Chapter Principals must be Past Masters in Craft. By introducing an 'authorised' way of sharing the work around, it's easy to organise the Ceremonies, involve more people, and achieve a better and more interesting end result. Of course the transition is taking time, partially because more experienced Companions are often loathe to let go of the familiar Ritual (which they may have taken years to learn) and start again with new Work. Some Chapters are not utilising the PAV Ceremonies, which is completely fine if it doesn't impact their recruitment and development progress. However the PAV is a good retention tool for smaller Chapters who are not so fortunate with their Candidate flow.

Chapter Ritual progresses in a different way to Craft. The set-up of Officers is such that the main Working Offices, MEZ (First Principal) and PS, can usually only be reached by passing through two Assistant offices associated with each. So, if you are lucky enough to be in a Chapter where progression through the offices is linear, you will have two years at each 'end' of the Temple during which you will be assisting these two Officers with the major Ceremonies, giving you ample time to observe and absorb the more substantial Work before you are called upon to perform it yourself.

Another difference is the amount and scale of the monologous Ritual in Chapter. Sure, there are some perambulations, particularly during the Exaltation of a new member, but the bulk of the learning you will have to do is in Lecture form. Both the PS and the three Principals have some long passages to learn and deliver.

Doubtless there are many remarkable human beings who can effortlessly memorise and regurgitate long passages of awkward English prose. They are, however, in the minority. Plus, an even smaller minority is comprised of those who can not only remember the Work, but also deliver it with style and character, so that it's interesting for the audience and particularly for the Candidate.

Just as in the Craft, most Chapter Ritual is directed at a Candidate who is usually hearing it for the first time, and who will make a judgment about his engagement with the Order based in part on how he engages with the Ritual being directed his way.

So, here are the two basic rules of good Ritual;

1. You need to know your stuff.
2. You cannot be boring.

Lucky for you that you have this Book to guide you!

The Purpose of the Ritual

Many authors have written eloquently on the subject of Masonic Ritual and its delivery in the Temple. Almost without exception, they state that the primary purpose of the Ritual is to *teach* the Candidate. Whilst this is a noble sentiment, and is indeed a part of the grand design of Masonry which is to educate, maybe it's a good idea to turn around the telescope and a look into it from the other end!

How receptive is the Candidate likely to be?

In reality, when a Candidate offers himself for Exaltation, he's probably a bit nervous. Of course (and we've all said this to a trembling initiate at one time or another) every Brother or Companion starts from the same position, and later in our Masonic careers we come to understand the purposes and procedures of the Ceremonies. Sitting on the backbenches, or from the relative safety of a Principal Officer's chair, we have time to observe and absorb the Ritual when it's being performed by someone else. There's no pressure on us.

You might think that in Chapter, it would be different for the Exaltee, because he's already passed through the experiences of the Three Craft Degrees. Maybe for some that is true, but experience shows that even mature Brethren who come late to the Royal Arch are often still highly apprehensive when it comes to their Exaltation!

Unless he's been illicitly briefed in advance, the Exaltee has absolutely no idea about what is happening, especially since for a substantial part of the Ceremony his vision is obscured, and is relying wholly on sound and touch to interpret what is going on around him.

Benevolent sensory deprivation is designed to confuse and disorientate the Candidate, so it's hard to believe, no matter how well the Ritual Ceremony is delivered, that the poor guy is actually in a position to learn anything at all!

What is actually imparted is an overall impression of Royal Arch Masonry, with all its intricacies.

So, if we accept that the objective of actually educating the Candidate will be very hard to achieve, what are the next most important priorities of a well-delivered Ceremony?

It's All About a Smooth Meeting

Whilst it may be true that the original purpose of the Ritual is to educate the Candidate, in reality it is the wholeness of the Ceremony that will be remembered by most everyone in the Chapter. The smoothness, consistency and demeanour with which it is conducted, the accuracy and conformity to the 'Book', and the pleasure and satisfaction which result from good Teamwork, will matter far more to the Companions. It simply makes for a better meeting.

For the Candidate, he is in no position to judge many of the elements. His impressions will be derived from the firm and secure way that he is handled by the PS. In practical terms, this is more important for the Candidate's favourable impression of the Chapter than any minor success he may have in deciphering the language and absorbing the lessons!

The Candidate will have plenty of time to observe the Ceremonies in the future. What's most important is that the working Officers achieve a level of competence and confidence which ultimately delivers a satisfactory Ceremony for the benefit of everyone present in the Temple.

Channelling Your Inner Actor!

Other authors on Ritual urge the reader to channel their "inner-actor". This is wise advice; however it is unlikely to work for everyone. Masons are drawn from every walk of life and it is not a natural component of human nature to be able to *act* in a convincing way. During my years in Masonry I have been fortunate to observe some truly amazing Ritualists, who are able to perform the Ceremony almost as a piece of entertainment. Most "ordinary" Lodges and Chapters are predominantly made up of members who do not possess this theatrical bent.

Maybe Ritual is more like a business presentation than a theatrical performance. When you stand up in the Chapter, you are setting out to demonstrate your expertise in a particular subject (the Ritual), whilst holding the audience's attention. In business, the stakes are often high, so the pressure to perform is real. Many more of us will experience this real-life business situation than will ever give a theatrical performance.

It's only human nature to want to be liked and respected, however Masonry implies a certain restraint, a balance if you like. Over-the-top, theatrical ritual may sometimes be counter-productive to your relationship with the other Members. Words like 'modest' and 'demeanour' crop up time and time again in Masonry for good reason.

Great Ritual is all about striking a balance between your own competence and capabilities, and the environment in which you are called upon to "perform". It might be described as a cross between 'camouflage' and 'context'.

Later we will discuss the various techniques such as metering, intonation, rhythm and posture which go together to achieve a balanced delivery. What matters most, once the techniques are in place, is Sincerity. This is a much more natural way to deliver the Ceremony, but of course it requires you to internalise a certain amount of empathy and understanding of the Ritual that you're delivering. As you will learn later, this skill is not difficult to acquire.

Shoulders Back, Chest Out...

Only around one third of everyday communication is purely verbal. Broad-channel communication, as any public speaker or presenter knows, is only achieved visually and emotionally when the body language is right. Some writers have gone to great lengths and describe in great detail the posture that you should adopt whilst delivering Ritual, particularly Lectures. This is highly subjective, and although it may be great to be able to puff up your chest, hold total eye contact, and control the movement of your hands in concert with the delivery of the vocal element, this mastery will take time to develop.

In your early days, you just need to find your own comfort zone as regards posture, movement, and gesticulation. As a Ritualist, you will benefit a lot if you can 'centre' yourself.

When you are delivering a two-thousand word monologue in front of knowledgeable and critical audience, you'll have enough to think about without having to worry about how you look. So you will find later in the book that we'll focus more on relaxation as a means of achieving confidence and competent delivery, rather than precise positioning. With the right techniques, relaxation is a state which is achievable under almost any circumstances, and there are tricks and tips which will enable you to convert nervousness and stress into excitement and enthusiasm. After all, these are the same physical manifestations, but become positive or negative according to the context at the time.

How Royal Arch Ritual Works

As you should already have learned, typical Craft Ritual workings, dominated in England by Emulation and Taylors, with many variants such as West End, Logic, D.M Goudielock etc., revolve around the period during which the First Temple at Jerusalem was built by King Solomon around 957BC. The stories build from a peaceful and regal beginning which explains the inspiration for and construction of the Temple, leading up to a cataclysmic event which, in the minds of traditionalist scholars, gave rise to the birth of Speculative Freemasonry. Throughout this series of short 'plays', there are embedded dozens of metaphors, imparting the moral criteria which a Freemason is expected to aspire to.

The Royal Arch Ritual picks up again some 420 years later, long after the First Temple has been destroyed by the Babylonians, and deals with the period during the preparation to build the Second Temple at Jerusalem, on the original site of the First Temple. A series of enlightening archaeological discoveries are made concerning the First Temple which is of great significance to the central messages and traditions of Freemasonry.

Once again, the Ritual is composed of exquisitely crafted language, and for most Masons the messages go in and stay in, enabling them to live more positive and fulfilled lives.

Royal Arch Masonry and Religion

The subject of Masonry's relationship with Religion is constantly in view. It's hard to avoid the perception of parts of the outside world that there are quasi-religious elements to Masonry. I have met dozens of great guys who have purposely avoided Masonry because they feel that it would be 'too religious' for them. It's rather ironic!

If you have no issues with attending a church wedding or funeral, or being a Godfather for someone's new baby, you will not meet any greater religious demands in Royal Arch Freemasonry. Masonry and its members respect religion, and are completely at ease with each other's beliefs, whatever they may be. Masons do not worship in Lodges or Chapters: that is the role of the Church.

Aside of our conventional Craft and Royal Arch orders, which are administered by the UGLE, there are numerous other Masonic Orders, many of which welcome those of a more religious inclination, such as the Rose Croix and the Knights Templars. That's your private business in the future.

At first glance, Royal Arch Masonry appears to have a more consistent religious thread running through it, however this definitely does not make it a religious Masonic Order. Whether or not one is devout, the Biblical stories which underpin Masonry are actually historical texts which describe the development of well-ordered societies, from which we all benefit today. The emphasis on religious belief in those times was probably more an indicator of mankind's needs to have a focus on reason. In ancient times, there was not the science available to explain much of what the world comprised, nor the human condition, so in the absence of other explanations, religious faith was the safety net which governed moral behaviour. Membership of Chapter demands no greater inclination than the non-specific 'belief in a Supreme Being' which qualified you for Masonry in the first place.

The obvious overlap between Religion and Freemasonry is Morality, which both teach as their primary function. The key difference in their approach is that fundamental religion tends towards 'God-Fearing Morality' whilst Masonry speaks more to the Moral Compass, and the idea that your behaviour in life should be geared towards preserving the stability of society and the happiness of everyone around you.

However, what is clear is that the historical basis for Royal Arch Ritual is largely grounded in the Old Testament of the King James Bible. If you are interested in exploring this aspect of Masonic Ceremonial origin further, there is an excellent book on the subject by Mike Neville, called "Sacred Secrets, Freemasonry, The Bible, and Christian Faith" which explains all the links throughout Craft and Royal Arch Masonry, and many of the other Allied Orders.

For the singular purpose of learning and executing Royal Arch Chapter Ritual, religion has no relevance whatsoever.

What this Book and it's methodology attempts to do, therefore, is to give the aspiring Ritualist a practical and pragmatic approach to the methods and skills needed to perform Ritual to an acceptable standard in the Chapter. It is taken as a given fact that you are a Freemason 'In Your Heart' and so it stays away from the moral aspects of Freemasonry.

And remember, everyone wants you to succeed!

So Why Do You Want To 'Do' Ritual?

We all meet great Ritualists during our Masonic Careers. Guys who make it look so easy, rattling off Tracing Boards and Mystical Lectures with one hand symbolically tied behind their back. To them, it seems so effortless, and to some of us, so daunting. Often, the common reaction is to defeat yourself before you even get started. You classify yourself as a 'non-Ritualist'.

That's a shame, because it really isn't so difficult if you have a system to follow.

Though many Chapters are over-subscribed and never short of Officers, there are many others, one of which you may be a member of, who either have just enough Candidates coming through to maintain a complete progression for the Offices, or worse, have too few Candidates and are forced to refill Offices with Past Principals on a regular basis. In these Chapters, there is sometimes justification for Candidates to leap-frog Offices because of expediency.

Hopefully your Chapter has a healthy attitude to bringing Candidates through the Offices and the associated Ritual and Ceremonies, so you will have many great years and many excellent opportunities to participate in the Work.

Even the smallest piece of well-delivered Ritual gives great satisfaction to the Companion concerned, and also to the rest of the Chapter.

So, if you've understood thus far, you should have a warm feeling about the value of Ritual to yourself and your Chapter, and hopefully some positive interest in learning the skills to take part.

Ritual Rewards

Once you have that warm feeling, it's only reasonable to look at the rewards that come with mastering the Work.

Your Masonic Legacy

Whenever anyone in my Lodge or Chapter mentions a Brother or Companion who has passed, they often tag him with "He was a Great Ritualist". It is remembered, as it is a little part of your legacy! If you join Masonry in mid-life, you will form multiple friendships that could endure for twenty or thirty years, which is a long time! These relationships matter in your life. You should aim to be respected in as many of your walks of life as possible, and Ritual is no different.

Competition for Offices

By involving yourself enthusiastically in the Work, you will raise your profile in the Chapter and you could improve your chances of being chosen for Office. This is important in Chapters where there is competition for offices.

Where Is It All Leading?

One day you will hopefully arrive at the MEZ's Chair, and your year as First Principal will be remembered largely on the basis of the way you conduct the Chapter Business.

The perfect MEZ's year scenario is that you have sufficient Candidates to ensure that you get to do at least one Exaltation, and two enthusiastic Principal successors to ensure that the Installation Meeting is a good one too.

Rewards for the Inner Man

They say that "Politics is Showbiz for Ugly People". For the rest of us there's Masonry!

Ritual's primary purpose is to implant the moral metaphors of Masonic teaching. Unequivocal. Put it aside.

For the purposes of this Book, we're concentrating on two main factors;

Firstly, how your Ritual performance will enhance the well-being of your Chapter, and secondly how it makes you feel. When you do your Work in the Temple, you will probably experience a profound sense of achievement every time you take on something challenging and deliver it well.

Engagement, Understanding, and Enjoyment – The Virtuous Circle

You will develop a greater understanding of the meaning of Royal Arch Masonry, indeed Masonry in general, and you'll have a more inclusive experience at Chapter meetings. You'll be 'part of the action' which is a lot more interesting and stimulating that falling asleep through boredom from the side-lines. Almoners Reports, Charity Stewards Reports, Treasurers Reports, the Risings and so on, whilst a necessary and integral part of the Chapter Business, can be awfully tedious if that's all you do at the meeting.

Many people don't get involved because they lack confidence. For those that have it, it's hard to understand. Everyone gets nervous, but some people just accept it as a limitation and never get to experience the thrill and stimulus of performance. If you are one of those who feel overwhelmed and challenged on the confidence front, all I ask is that you first accept that there might be a way through it for you, so that you can join the ranks of those who get a little excitement or satisfaction from giving it a try.

Enhancing Your Communication Skills

If you put in the work, which is almost guaranteed to be a positive experience once you commit to it, your public communication skills, particularly in business, will be significantly enhanced by your new confidence and calmness in front of an audience.

The Toolbox of Techniques

If you are prepared to put in a little time and stick to the structured process, this Book will provide you with a toolbox of techniques. Most people have the basic intellectual ability to do quite complex things, but many fall short because they lack a system or the guidance to apply their resources in a structured way.

I have met many Freemasons on my travels who are highly intelligent professionals in their work-life and are indeed competent at multiple skills requiring immense intellectual capability, but nevertheless fall short when it comes to the Ritual. They often appear to be baffled by their inability to master what is a relatively simple task, and this serves to reinforce my observation that, although they are quite capable of doing this, they simply are not approaching it in the right way.

Quite a few of them appear to be of the belief that if you read something enough times it will magically enter your brain, lodge there, and simply deliver itself on demand, perfectly. This is the "it'll be all right on the night" school of Masonic Ritual. It rarely works.

Others I have met are in possession of the basic tools and techniques, and may indeed be quite eloquent once they are on their feet in the Chapter, but invariably simply do not allow themselves enough time in the run-up to the meeting. It is indeed possible to 'learn' a short Ceremony in a matter of a few days, but when it comes to the delivery you will be working from short-term memory alone, and this introduces a significant performance risk. Learning Ritual is not just about being able to memorise things.

So, I hope that this preamble has got you thinking, and perhaps it's stimulated your curiosity to go a little bit further.

Chapter Survival

My own Chapter struggled with membership numbers for many years. It usually met on a Wednesday at around 4pm in Central London. At one point, things were looking so bad that we even considered amalgamation, or handing back the Warrant (a drastic solution under any circumstances).

The key problem was identified as the timing. As the membership profile evolved, and less of the members worked or lived in Greater London, they simply couldn't justify a day off work, perhaps an overnight hotel stay, or the high cost of travel to attend the meetings.

Miraculously, a simple solution was suggested, which was to move the meeting to Saturday Morning, on the same day as our Craft Meetings in the afternoon. We eliminated the extra Festive Board, and because most of the Chapter Members were also members of two Saturday Lodges with which we aligned the Chapter Meetings, there was no incremental travel cost to attend. Everyone just needed to get up earlier!

The date switch took around 18 months to effect, mainly because Freemasons Hall is very full most Saturdays, but we eventually pulled it off, and both the membership and the quality of the Meetings and Ceremonies has consistently improved ever since. People who had not been to Chapter for several years started to drift back, new Candidates have regularly appeared, and even the General Fund is back in the black. There is renewed enthusiasm, not least from the VO, and this Chapter has been saved. It wouldn't work for every struggling

Chapter, but it worked for ours!

Chapter 2

The Challenges of Chapter Ritual

Some People Make It Look So Easy!

In essence, there's not much difference between Craft and Chapter Ritual. You learn it, you deliver it, everyone pats you on the back and you move on. So why do so many apparently capable people find it so terribly daunting?

There are plenty of Royal Arch Masons who have acquired or developed the skills to manage their Ritual without too many obstacles. Some people are naturally talented at this. I wouldn't say 'gifted', because if you ask these guys how they do it, they'll tell you that it's a lot of hard work to achieve a good standard, but they have systems and processes that work for them.

If you have tried learning any kind of Ritual and have come up against obstacles stopping you from getting to this standard, it's likely that you fall into one of two categories;

- You don't have a reliable system for learning, and/or

- You struggle with your confidence.

The Secret Weapons of Great Ritualists

Allowing Enough Time

The first and most important reason why people fail is because they don't allow anywhere near enough time. Later in the book I will give you estimations of the amount of time needed to master each component of a Royal Arch Ceremony. Although many Chapters do hold Chapter of Improvement meetings, similar to the Craft Lodge of Instruction, in lots of others the Chapter rehearsals come a distant second to the priorities of the Lodge. You may, if you are particularly unfortunate, have no access whatsoever to a Chapter of Improvement. We'll try to cover every eventuality, so that even if you rarely get to rehearse, you'll nevertheless learn the techniques and tools to do a good job.

When starting to learn Chapter Ceremonies, many people tend to think in terms of weeks, whereas you should really be thinking in terms of months. This the main reason why people struggle to cross the finishing line in time for the meeting. It is the most important factor.

Masonry, by most definitions, is a hobby. The difference between Masonry and other 'hobbies' is that Masonry has deadlines.

Think of it in terms of Premier League Football. The great teams usually have very fit players, who peak at exactly the right time for each important game. Let's imagine that another team may not be as astute at delivering peak fitness on match days. So their players turn up for the game only 80% physically and mentally prepared. That

20% gap will often be the difference that decides the match.

The objective of good time-planning is to get yourself to a peak of competence exactly when you need to be there, on the day of the Meeting. This needs a long-view, and an honest reality-check at the start. Learning Ritual is not really an art, it's more like a science. It cries out for process. If you make a reasonably accurate timetable, starting as soon as you know what is required of you, and stick to the process, you will succeed.

Different Kinds of Time

At the risk of repetition, the Number One reason why people mess up Ritual is because they underestimate the amount of time needed. In extreme cases, some people think that they can pick up the Book the night before and that by reading it through a few times, it will magically stick.

It doesn't work.

Even if you appreciate that much more time is required, not all time is created equal!. You might be led to believe, for instance, that it will typically take twenty hours to learn a Lecture to a competent standard. By extension, you might therefore conclude that three hours a day for the week before the meeting will have you right there on the day.

This would be a mistake for most people, mainly because nobody can possibly focus on a single task for three hours every day! But the second dimension is this; learning is a distillation process. Active concentration on the task is only part of the process. To learn effectively, to 'distil' something properly, there's a lot going on in the background.

So the same twenty hours, consumed at a slower rate, will be much more effective. Twenty minutes a day, spread over two months, is a much more reliable method. In truth, twenty minutes of active participation in the learning task is likely to result in three or four times that in passive learning (cooking) which will take place in your subconscious without any noticeable effort.

Good Learning Technique

To repeat, TIME is the most important ingredient of learning and delivering good Ritual. If you were to stop reading this book right now (please don't) you have already learned the most important lesson.

The second reason why people fall short is because they employ ineffective learning techniques.

Audio Recording – Just Say No

There's one technique which most Masons try at some time, because it's such a blatantly obvious short-cut, and that's Audio Recording.

A few years ago, some Masonic Ceremonies were commercially available on CD's. However, these seem to have completely disappeared now, apart from some unauthorised items. QED.

I would be a hypocrite if I said that Audio Recording has no place in this process. I sometimes use it to check myself against a written copy. It's an easy way to spot where you are habitually going wrong. Its application at the back-end of the learning process might be useful for some people, copyright notwithstanding!

However, the idea that repeatedly listening to a recording of a Ceremony is going to magically work for you is, in most cases, a blind alley. From my own trials and experiments, and those of others I have spoken to, this method tends to fail when the pressure is on. Relying on your auditory sense to implant the sequences and language of the Ritual in your mind, and enable them for recall, is a risky business.

There's another thing about Audio Recording, which I've heard from quite a number of Masons. It's sort of Taboo.

My interpretation of the 'Secrets' is that they are words that are never written out longhand, especially in the Ritual book. The rest of the Ritual is just written language, which is available to anyone, so if you re-write part of it to make it more portable, such as a smartphone or Kindle, although you must pay due respect to any copyright issues, you aren't breaching any of your Obligations of Secrecy.

But there's something about Audio Recording that sometimes makes it feel like cheating. Or at least it feels like that to me. That's why I usually don't include it in my learning system.

Good Ritualists have a tool-box of learning techniques. Some are common to everybody, and these are the ones we'll develop in the next few Chapters, because anyone should be able to master them quickly.

More subtle are the unique, customised techniques that Ritualists use, according to their own experiences. Once you start attending Chapter of Improvement and talking to other Masons about Ritual, you will be offered lots of different things to try. You should explore all you can.

Get Lost… In The Language

Another challenge which many aspiring Ritualists must face is the commitment required to become immersed in the Ritual passage you are trying to learn. The Ritual language is peppered with patterns, alliteration and links which can be smartly harnessed to aid the important Memory Recall process which is part of the performance package you're going to learn.

The Work is packed full of imagery, memory cues, patterns and clues to help you learn it and deliver it well. Many Masons never discover these aids because they simply view the passage as a succession of words and sentences.

In this sense I'm talking only about the language used, not the meaning of the story. 'Understanding' the Ritual is a big subject all of its own, which is covered more fully later in the book.

Bite Sized Pieces

Another set of attributes which are 'designed-in' to the Ritual are natural break points. As a quick demonstration of this, try the following exercise;

1. On your PC's word processor, type in (copy) the Ritual passage you are learning now, or next. If it's a really long one, just do a couple of pages. Make sure you type in the punctuation accurately.
2. Next, use the Return key to break the passage down into mini-paragraphs of no more than three sentences (only one or two if they're long ones).

3. Now use the numbering tool to automatically number each paragraph.
4. Those numbers will tell you the number of 'sessions' you will need to commit the words to memory, following the system you'll learn in this book. In the original 'Learning Masonic Ritual' we used these numbers to tell us how many DAYS we would need to memorize the first Stage of the process. However, it's important to recognize that the Chapter Ceremonies will be less familiar to most Masons, and more complex than the Craft Work. So, in this exercise, it will probably help to make these individual Sessions longer than a day, probably two or even three days per Session.

This simple exercise should have immediately introduced the idea of a systematic approach to learning your Work. We'll develop the techniques shortly, and you'll start to see the benefits immediately.

Breaking the whole into easy parts will speed up the learning process and give you clear milestones to measure your progress. It may seem obvious to you, but you'd be surprised how many people don't do it this way.

Anatomy of the Ritualist

The identifying characteristic of most decent Ritualists is Confidence. Many people are capable of learning complex and demanding passages from the Ritual book, but hold themselves back because they lack the confidence to deliver the end-result. Having this obstacle in the road ahead, no matter how distant, induces self-defeat right at the outset. Simply put; "I won't be able to do this on the day, so what's the point in trying to learn it?"

The Ritualist has probably been there, but got past it. So will you, if you follow the system and believe in your inherent ability to do things you've never tried before, if you're shown the right techniques. It's called Learning, but it's just as much about Growing.

Ritual Home Truths

The truth about Ritual is this; there's no magic bullet! Most people who can 'do it' have simply discovered the right combination of memorizing technique and hard work to get them to a standard where they feel comfortable and can acquit themselves satisfactorily.

So the objective of this book is to encourage and assist Royal Arch Masons who may be on their way up through the Offices to prepare to be able to do their Principal's work themselves, once the time comes.

In the Craft you'll generally have a minimum of seven or eight years from Initiation to Installation. Unless your Chapter is over-subscribed, it's possible that you could be heading to the East much faster, possibly as quickly as two or three years from Exaltation to Third Principal. Nevertheless this still presents you with lots of opportunities to learn, practice, and prepare to be the Ritualist that lurks inside all of us!

Don't Expect Instant Enlightenment!

In Chapter, there is only one Ceremony (your Exaltation) before you will be given your Ritual Book (hereinafter, the 'Book'). You might take it home and put it in a drawer and come back to it some years later, which would be a shame. You might try to read it, and realize, like many things in your Masonic journey, it doesn't mean much to you, especially since a lot of the words are blanked out or abbreviated.

Don't worry! Nobody 'gets it' first time. It *is* confusing, it's *meant* to be that way. Chapter Ritual is arguably even more enigmatic than Craft Ritual (Masonry being a progressive science) but you should not be put off by this. The more challenging the Ritual, the more enjoyable it is once you master it.

Masonry encourages you to question everything you see and hear, and soon it will start to form structures and patterns which will develop your understanding of what's going on behind the scenes. Because principally, Masonry is just a big collection of metaphors for life, and the Ceremonies and Rituals contained in the little Book are just stories, acted out in the Chapter to provide a delivery mechanism for the messages of morality to be conveyed and implanted.

Of course this may not strike you in the early years. At first, the Book can seem like Double-Dutch. And even when you first encounter the Ritual Ceremonies in the Chapter, they may not make much sense to you either. As I said before, it takes time to form itself into a structure; remember the Third Degree Craft Ceremony talks about 'the connection of our whole system and the relative dependence of its several parts' and eventually things will become clearer.

By attacking every opportunity to learn and deliver new Ritual, you will begin to understand how it all fits together, and that will supercharge your enjoyment of being in the Chapter.

The Basics

Here are some basics, and I apologise if you are already well past this stage. It's an explanation of how the Chapter Offices progress, the particular skill sets that you need for each one, and the variances between them. If you're already heading for the Chairs and you know all this stuff, please feel free to skip to the next section.

The Offices and How They Work

In general, the two hardest-working Offices in the Royal Arch Chapter are the First Principal ('Z') and the Principal Sojourner (P.S.).

PS

It's likely that your first taste of Office in Chapter will be as either 2nd Assistant or 1st Assistant Sojourner. The former of these offices doesn't have much to do, and very little to learn, so if you are in that office, you are ideally placed to observe the order of events during the Chapter Ceremonies. Keep your eyes on the PS, because you could find yourself doing that job within one or two years, and it is a substantial ceremonial position.

The 1st AS is more involved, particularly during the Exaltation Ceremony, when he has perambulations to follow with the PS and the Candidate. Again, understudying the PS work during your year as 1st AS is important, because it will probably be your turn next.

Once you become PS, you are in the spotlight. As mentioned elsewhere, there are really only two Ceremonies in the Chapter calendar, which are Exaltation (the initiation of a new Member) and the Installation (the change-over of the three Principal Offices). As PS, apart from the minor participation in the Opening and Closing Ceremonies, you should be focused on the Exaltation Ceremony, because most of that Ceremony is performed by yourself and the First Principal. We will look in detail at the PS Work at Exaltation further on in the book.

Scribe N

In many Chapters, Scribe N is one of those offices traditionally occupied by a Past Principle, and you will not pass through it on your way to the East. In terms of Ritual, Scribe N is a very important part of all the Ceremonies, and actively assists in many aspects. However, there isn't much Ritual prose for Scribe N to learn, as most of his work involves perambulations.

Third Principal, 'J', and Second Principal, 'H'

For both these Officers, there are four main elements to their Work in the Chapter. Firstly, the Opening and Closing Ceremonies, which involve perambulations and a few short words. Secondly, the Installation of their successors as they are promoted to the next Principals Chair. Thirdly, the 'Robes and Sceptres' Lectures at the Installation, which are relatively short and quick to learn. Finally, and most challenging, are the Principal's Lectures, performed at Exaltation.

Neither the Third Principal's (the Historical) Lecture, nor the Second Principal's (the Symbolical) Lecture is compulsory at the Exaltation Ceremony, and it is not unusual to see one or both of them missed out. This is a shame, because they are quite important in the context of a new Candidate's understanding of Royal Arch Masonry. Neither is more than five minutes long, so any excuse that there isn't enough time is usually flawed. More often, particularly in small Chapters, is that the Officer concerned has not been able to learn the Lecture, possibly because of Ritual overload elsewhere, and this provides an ideal opportunity for a new Companion or Novice Ritualist to step in and do this Work. It is important to note that these Lectures do NOT have to be given by a Principal, either current or past, and can be allocated to any competent Companion in the Chapter.

The First Principal, 'MEZ'

MEZ (or simply 'Z') is the 'equivalent' of the WM in Craft, and is the Boss (although Scribe 'E' may disagree). The work-load for Z is substantial, both in the Exaltation and Installation Ceremonies. There is the assumption that Z has served in PS, 3rd and 2nd Principal Offices on the way to his Chair, and therefore is capable and willing to take on the major Ceremonies as they fall to him. Until you are installed as First Principal, you cannot be 'delegated' any of that work EXCEPT it is quite permissible for any competent Companion to deliver either part or all of the Mystical Lecture. For the novice Ritualist, the Permitted Alternative Version is split into three digestible parts which are relatively short but nevertheless challenging. In the original form, the Mystical Lecture is a substantial undertaking and not recommended until you have progressed through at least the PS office.

The Other Offices

Once you have passed through the Principal's Chairs, you will serve one year as IPZ and then you may be considered for Secretary (Scribe E), Treasurer, Director of Ceremonies etc. In a small Chapter it's possible that you will find yourself 'recycled' back to an earlier office, which is why this Ritual Learning System places great emphasis on maintaining the Ceremonies you learned on your first ascent, for re-use in the future!

Although there are many similarities and parallels in Chapter to Craft, the main difference with the Royal Arch is that the PS Office plays a much more important role in the proceedings much earlier in the progression. It is a supercharged hybrid of JD and SD in Craft, and you could be in the PS Office in a very short space of time after you first join Chapter. From there, it might only be three or four years before you are sitting in the First Principal's Chair (depending on the competition for offices in your Chapter), so it's entirely feasible that you could be First Principal of your Chapter before you are Master of your Lodge! Four or five years sounds like a long time, but if you only meet three times a year that's about a fortnight of afternoons and boozy suppers! Luckily it's spread out over time, and in Ritual terms it's actually the time *between* the meetings that's most important.

Nevertheless, there's a lot to learn, so we'd better crack on....

Chapter 3
Making Your Plan

Measuring the Work

In this Chapter, we're going to learn how to 'Measure the Work'. That means estimating the task ahead and setting up a schedule to ensure you achieve your aims.

The first time you learn a new piece of Work, it will be challenging and it will take time. However, a well-considered and well-constructed plan will carry most of your load, provided you stick to it.

Obviously the more time you can allow yourself, the better you will do. But if you do it properly, the next time you come back to do it again it will be much simpler to revise and polish. In fact, you will probably become very good at this.

Go and Watch a Ceremony Before You Learn It

When you are sitting in a Chapter, and you watch a Ceremony being performed, it's quite hard to fathom how that complex piece of Masonic theatre could possibly be condensed into twenty or thirty pages of that tiny Book in your pocket.

The truth is, it isn't!

In English Craft and Royal Arch Masonry, the Book is

really just a guide to the protocol and language. It's really not practical to try to learn a Ceremony, particularly one which involves multiple participants and perambulations, simply by using the Book as a script. Ritual is so much more than that, and much of the fabric of the Ceremony is implicit knowledge, transmitted from Mason to Mason over time.

In this respect, the Chapter of Improvement, if available to you, is invaluable. However as a starting point for your first Ceremony, there's no substitute for seeing a live 'performance'.

For example; If you have never seen an Exaltation Ceremony (remember, you didn't get to see a great deal during your own) you must arrange to see at least one or two whilst you're learning the PS's work. You should arrange to go as soon as you can, so that you get a clear picture of the floor-work. Nobody will mind if you make notes on the back of your summons, or sketch a drawing, but it will really help to give the Ritual some context once you dive into the Book.

I have checked. There are no training videos on YouTube!

Visiting Other Chapters

Visiting is often called the 'Life Blood of Freemasonry', and some of the members of your Chapter will be regular visitors to other Chapters. Ask around, and it's almost certain that someone will be overjoyed to take you along to another meeting where you can see what you need to see.

All Lodges and Chapters welcome visitors. Just ask the Scribe E of your Chapter to suggest one or two friendly Chapters that you could contact, and e-mail their

Secretaries. Or ask your Chapter Janitor or Lodge Tyler, who will know what each of his Chapters is doing in the coming weeks. But please try to find a way to see the Ceremony you are learning early on. It will make a huge difference to your initial progress to put the whole thing into context at the beginning.

If you're in or near London, both Aldersgate and Domatic Chapters of Improvement are held weekly at Freemasons Hall. Full details of their meeting dates and times can be found on the Metropolitan Grand Lodge & Grand Chapter Website at **www.porchway.org**.

The Learning System

Earlier in the Book, you found out that the key reason why people struggle with Ritual is that they don't have a structured process to follow, including allowing the right amount of time. In this section, you will learn a System to take care of this.

We are going to focus on Three Stages in a Process, which, when correctly followed, will ensure you reach your optimum performance standard just before your 'Target Meeting'.

The Three Stages are these;

Stage One: Cramming

In this stage, you are going to focus on memorizing the text of your Work, as quickly as possible, to around 85% accuracy. The objective of Stage One is to take you to a position where you can recite the Work all the way through, without stopping, even if it is a little inaccurate.

The idea is that you will quickly acquire enough knowledge to be able to understand the language and the flow of the Ceremony, which will give you a solid launch-pad from which to propel yourself through the next two stages.

Stage Two: Polishing

In this stage, you are going to take the Work you have memorised in Stage One, and start to correct your errors, using some techniques which you will learn shortly, whilst the Ceremony embeds itself in your long term memory. You will be using some of your subconscious abilities to really 'learn' the Work, so that you can then begin to concentrate on the Performance and Delivery aspects.

Stage Three: Rehearsal

In this stage, you will have memorised and learned both the Work and the some of the meanings behind it, and now you will start to focus on 'performing' it, which will enable you to discover many of the inbuilt rhythms and patterns in the Ceremony. By tying all these strands together, you will gain both confidence and competence. You can expect to arrive at a point where you are in possession of all the attributes to deliver an excellent performance in the Meeting.

In order to allocate these three Stages correctly, we first need to look at the Time-Line.

Planning the Work

In Craft Masonry, you will be familiar with the four main Ceremonies, which are the three Degrees and the Installation. With their associated Lectures and Charges, more frequent meetings, as well as the (usually) larger memberships in Lodges than Chapters, Craft Lodges provide plenty of opportunity to learn and deliver new and different Ritual on a regular basis.

Conversely, Royal Arch Masonry has only two main Ceremonies, namely Exaltation and Installation. The Exaltation Ceremony places most of the Work squarely on the shoulders of the PS and the First Principal, however the relatively recent inclusion of the Permitted Alternative Versions of the Ritual does allow for participation by other Candidates, and indeed even the most challenging piece, the Mystical Lecture, is now authorised to be performed by any 'Competent Companion', who need not necessarily have passed through any of the Principal's Chairs.

PS Work at Exaltation

We will examine the PS work at Exaltation in detail later. However it is useful to have an overview of your part (as PS) in this important Ceremony, and in particular how to remember and practice the associated floor-work.

The PS work at Exaltation is the singular most important piece of work that any Royal Arch Mason will perform before reaching the Principal's Chairs. It involves some substantial dialogue with the First Principal, however in the first instance we are concerned with the Floor Work

(Perambulations) which form the critical part of the Exaltation itself. It's the first Ceremony in which you will play a pivotal role, so it carries some performance pressure. Secondly, and more importantly, it involves the first experience of a new Candidate in Royal Arch Masonry, which adds even more pressure. So it's in everyone's best interests that you get it right.

For the PS, this Ceremony has four main elements, as follows;

1. Entrusting the Candidate: for this you will leave the Temple, and since it's the Candidate's first encounter with Royal Arch Masonry, you need to be slick and rehearsed. The only other person who can help you with prompts is the Janitor.

2. The Exaltation Ceremony: in your role as PS, you will be in control of the Candidate throughout this part, similarly to a Working Deacon in Craft. There are a few words to learn, specifically for the raising of the Candidate, but everything else in this part of the Ceremony involves your actions and perambulations and instructing the Candidate to perform the actions required of him. You should apply all the techniques explained here, in particular you really need to watch this Ceremony at least once or twice before you try it for yourself, and Chapter of Improvement is strongly recommended for you to rehearse it.

3. Three MMs from Babylon: this section is a dialogue with the MEZ, who will ask you questions which you must answer according to the Ritual Book. You have

one monologue of around 260 words ("We would scorn to be descended...") which is central to this section. There are no significant perambulations beyond the entry and exit.

4. The Return of the Sojourners; this is the climax of the Ceremony and the biggest of your 'performances'. It begins with a 600 word Lecture and transitions to a series of perambulations which you will perform with other Chapter Officers.

Here, we are concerned with Section 2, which contains most of the Floor Work. For the new PS, it's really important and very useful to break down the floor-work into its constituent parts and simplify it into stages, so you can understand and more easily memorise the sequence of events. Don't be over-awed by what you may see. It really isn't as complicated as you think.

The main elements of Section 2 of the Exaltation are as follows;

- Admission and collection of the Candidate, conducting him to the W.
- Questions of examination, the Prayer
- Conducting the Candidate around the Chapter
- Advancing the Candidate to the KS
- The Vault, the Scroll
- The Obligation
- The Raising of the Candidate
- Reading the Scrl.
- Retiring the Candidate

Each of these elements can be further deconstructed into the individual actions, and represented as a diagram, an example of which is shown below. To be clear, using diagrams in this way is meant only as an aid to practising the work. Your aim should be to dispose of these diagrams as soon as you are confident that you have understood the sequence of the Ceremony and your position at each stage.

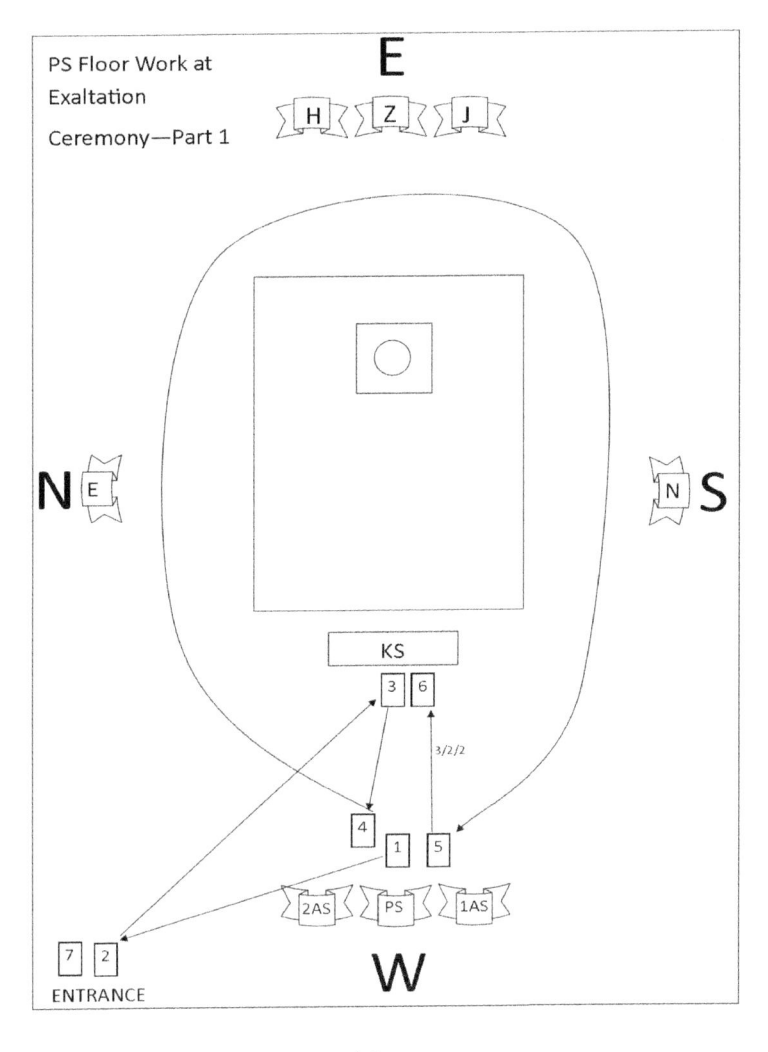

PS Floor Work at Exaltation
Ceremony—Part 1

E

H Z J

N E

N S

KS

3 6

3/2/2

4
1 5

2AS PS 1AS

7 2
ENTRANCE

W

~ 49 ~

In the example, the arrowed lines show your perambulations, and each numbered position corresponds with a section of Ritual. The best way to marry the Book and the Perambulations Diagram together is to mark each number in the appropriate place in the margin of your Ritual Book.

Time Planning for PS at Exaltation

In terms of timetable planning for the PS work in the Exaltation Ceremonies, I would recommend three to four months as ideal. This is not really based on your own learning ability, but simply to allow the maximum number of practice sessions with the rest of the Team. Your timetable will largely be dictated by the Chapter of Improvement schedule, however if you have any concerns that the CoI is making assumptions (i.e. not getting started on the work early enough for you), you should politely raise your concerns with either the Preceptor or the First Principal, who should understand. In any case, there's nothing to stop you getting started on the work yourself, either alone, or with the assistance of a nearby friendly Companion!

Learning the PS 'words' is done using exactly the systems and processes that you will learn in the next few chapters. The PS's Ritual passages are lengthy, and there are three of them. As long as you set out your timetable clearly at the beginning, you will have no problem in getting the words right on the day.

This learning system is all about systemising and structuring the process, and that includes using Learning Aids which force you to stick to the disciplines necessary to build up to a great performance. One of the most important and easily available of these is your cellphone, and in particular the sophisticated alarm and reminder functions that it has. Great Ritual comes from regular repetition in the rehearsal phase, and setting up daily alarms and reminders in your phone is a really easy and free way to ensure that you never forget to practice.

In addition, weekly checklists to track your rehearsal progress are also useful (example below). You can easily make these in Word or Excel, and either set them up on your PC, Tablet or Smartphone, and/or print them out and stick them in the back of your notebook, carry them in your wallet, or in your back pocket. Just check each box as many times as you practice the relevant section. This is an essential discipline, because it quickly gives you a visual representation of where you are focusing your rehearsal effort, and you can see if you are not paying enough attention to particular sections.

EXAMPLE REHEARSAL WEEKLY CHECKLIST – PS WORK AT EXALTATION

	Mo	Tu	We	Th	Fr
Opening the Chapter					
Entrusting the Candidate					
Floorwork, Steps & Obligation					
3 MM's from Babylon					
Return of Sojourners Dialog					
Investiture Floorwork					
Closing the Chapter					

All these little novelties may sound a bit twee; however they are just some of the Secret Weapons used by successful Ritualists, so you have nothing to lose by giving them a try.

There's not much more to say about floor-work. There are lots of ways of learning Ritual prose, but there's really only one way to achieve a high standard of floor-work, and that's Practice. The perambulations are taught, rather than learned.

The Lectures

Apart from the PS work, virtually all the other Ritual challenges in Chapter are in 'Lecture' form, meaning that the bulk of the Work can be learned alone.

The reason why these are separated is this; the PS's Exaltation work involves being part of a Team, which puts a heavier dependence on the Rehearsal phase (Stage Three) and the role of Chapter of Improvement.

Conversely, the 'Lectures' are just that, and can be very effectively learned and practiced without much outside help.

You will inevitably get very bored with the notion that 'Time Is of The Essence' as it's a recurring theme throughout this book. But it really is the critical factor, so setting up a workable timetable at the beginning of the process is simply unavoidable.

Calculating Your Time-Line

When you set about learning a Lecture, the recommended split for each of the 3 Stages is in the ratio of 2:1:1, in other words

- 2 Units of Time for Cramming
- 1 Unit of Time for Polishing
- 1 Unit of Time for Rehearsing

In order to calculate the total length of time required achieve performance-grade for any Lecture you therefore need to calculate the length of time for Stage One – Cramming - and double it.

This is done by breaking down the Lecture into sentences or passages (sections) that you can learn at a fixed speed, then numbering those pieces. You were shown a method for doing this earlier.

As previously mentioned, in Learning Masonic Ritual (Craft) we allocated one day for each section. In the Royal Arch, because a lot of the language is less intuitive, and less familiar, each section is nominally given two days in the Cramming Stage. Once you have broken down your piece, and doubled the total number i.e. two days per Section), that is the number of days you will need for Stage One, and from that you can easily calculate Stages Two and Three, and the scale of the whole task.

Once again I apologise if this simplistic explanation seems banal or obvious, and indeed it probably is. However, the whole purpose of applying this method to your learning is to provide you with a structured process which you can adhere to in order to achieve the desired result, and whilst you might already know how to divide by fourteen and multiply by two, you may never have thought to apply it to Learning Ritual in the past, so please bear with it!

Equally, once you complete the process for the first time, and prove to yourself that it works, you will then be in a position to experiment with varying the ratios between the stages, the size of the sections you apply to Stage One, and so on. Years from now, you should still be applying the same basic principles, but the numbers could be very different for each person.

Because of the huge variation in learning abilities across the range of human beings, for the purpose of this exercise we will use a 'standard model' which is Me.

You'll find a list of all the Chapter Ceremonies in the Appendix, with estimates of the timetable you should initially use when learning them. Of course, you will be able to adjust these schedules to suit your own abilities, but until you try one or two you won't actually know what your abilities are, so I would urge you to apply the standard model in the first instance.

Throughout this book, we'll be using two examples; firstly the PS Work at Exaltation, which is the first major Ceremony that a Chapter Officer performs, and secondly the Third Principal's 'Historical' Lecture. This relatively short Lecture has two advantages for the novice Chapter Ritualist; first it is permitted (under the PAV rules) to be given by any competent Companion in the Chapter, i.e. not necessarily an Installed Principal, and secondly it is often overlooked at Exaltation Ceremonies so you shouldn't have too much difficulty in landing the job if you request it. In terms of the Ritual variation between Domatic and Aldersgate, the two most popular Royal Arch Ritual systems, these are negligible. If your Chapter meets under a different convention, for example Universal, Warwickshire or Polaris, you should easily be able to translate the learning system to suit your Chapter's Ceremonies.

The Historical Lecture is an ideal piece for the aspiring Ritualist, because not only is it beautifully written, containing many rhythms and cues, but it naturally breaks down into around twenty bite-sized 'chunks' which are the perfect size to be memorized in forty days at the rate of one every other day..

Applying the Three-Stage Process (CPR) explained earlier, and the Standard Model (yours truly) this works as follows;

1. Stage One (Cramming); 40 Days
2. Stage Two (Polishing); 20 Days
3. Stage Three (Rehearsing); 20 Days

So we will make a plan that involves learning the example to 'performance standard' in three months.

Even experienced Companions, who may have performed a passage numerous times, prefer a month or two to revise, especially if it's been a while. The common theme is this; Perfect Preparation Prevents Poor Performance. So Standing Committees, PZ and GP Meetings have an obligation to the Chapter to allocate work as early as it's reasonably possible to do so.

Milestones

The purpose of setting up a detailed Timetable at the beginning is to give yourself fixed points so that you can measure your progress.

Once you've 'locked in' to a precise plan, you've automatically created your milestones: targets to shoot for which will keep you on schedule to peak at the right time, the day of the Meeting.

Once you start, you'll soon find out if your milestones are realistic. You can adapt your on-going approach once you find out how fast it's working for you.

Understanding the Ritual

A lot has been written about this, and it is obviously important. But here we're mainly concerned with things that will enable to learn quickly and deliver competently, so your intimate relationship with the Work will only really gather momentum once you are through the first couple of performances.

Just like Craft Ritual, which is largely metaphorical, the messages behind the stories are the main elements of Masonic and moral improvement, rather than the stories themselves. The use of metaphors to deliver implicit benefits is a key plank of Neuro Linguistic Programming (NLP) and Hypnotherapy. Your powerful subconscious mind is very sophisticated in the way it deals with language, and is easily capable of extracting and applying the meanings behind metaphors.

However, Royal Arch Ritual is, particularly in the case of the Exaltation Ceremony, more theatrical. A quick trawl of the web will bring you to many explanations of the message behind Royal Arch Masonry, and you'll understand how it forms a progression from the Craft, and takes you into different areas of morality and (for some) spirituality.

Of course to try and decipher the meanings behind the Ritual is another science entirely, and really not relevant to what we are targeting here, which is the learning and delivery of the Ritual itself. Besides, we're concentrating on the *value of the language*, which more than stands up on its own.

There are Masons who, quite genuinely, will advise you that to deliver good Ritual, you need to fully engage with the underlying meaning of the ritual and understand it. In the Craft Ceremonies this is quite a traditionalist approach. In the Chapter examples used here, it is more appropriate to look at the story itself as a means to assimilating the meaning. In both cases, if we are going to retain our beautiful Ritual, and grow our Membership, I believe that we need to re-frame the Work so that younger men can engage with it.

So, the simple approach is to apply a minimum standard of understanding, sufficient to enable you to work through the process of learning the Work. Basically, if it makes sense to you when you read it through, you probably have enough understanding to get on with it!

The Chapter Exaltation Ceremony is a more obvious 'historical play'. The story it tells stands up on its own, without the necessity for too much interpretation.

Phew, I think that covers the preamble. Now it's time to get started on the Work.

Stage One - 'Cramming'

The 'First Regular Step' in this system of learning to perform Ritual involves 'Cramming' at the beginning, even if it's just a rough version of your work.

You can polish the language later (hardly anyone ever gets it 100% right) but it's important to quickly demonstrate to yourself that you can fit the bulk of the language around the Ceremony. For the PS, you simply need to concentrate on linking the passages of Ritual with well-executed perambulations and strong guidance for the confused, disoriented chap on your left hand side!

This initial Objective is to get yourself quickly to a situation where you can stumble right through the Ceremony in your head. If you can, towards the end of Stage One, you really need to go and see it done again, so it will all start to fit together. The techniques for this initial cramming are covered in Chapter 4.

Summary

- To start, find somewhere that you can go to watch a performance of the Ceremony you are learning.
- There are Three Key Stages; Cramming, Polishing, and Rehearsing (C.P.R.)

- For the PS's floor-work, break it down into sections. Use diagrams to help you rehearse the perambulations.
- Set up daily alarms on your cellphone to practice your words.
- Carry a rehearsal check-list to keep you on schedule.
- Break down the Lectures into small sections that you can memorise at a set rate. Count the sections, and multiply by four it for the total time you'll need before you perform it. If you can, add two weeks for contingencies.

Chapter 4
Learning and Memorising

Stage One - Cramming

In this Chapter, we will learn and practice some of the basic skills of memorising a Ceremony for the first time, and get you started. This method of learning uses a 'building block' approach, to ensure that you lay solid foundations in the beginning, then 'raise a superstructure' one step at a time. You can't expect to put the roof on until you've built the walls!

The primary objective is to 'Cram' the memorising task as quickly as possible in order to give yourself maximum time for Polishing the Work in Stage 2, and then Rehearsing the Delivery in Stage 3.

Lots of scientists and quite a few crackpots have attempted to explain how memory actually works, but the truth seems to be that we're not really sure. Recent studies appear to show that memory is actually a holistic process across the whole of the brain, which takes and processes feeds from different senses. The notion exists that it's something like a database; when something happens to you, the sensual inputs are split out and stored in their appropriate brain areas. So all the visual stuff gets stored in the sight area, the sounds go to the audio area, and various kinaesthetic strands such as temperature, texture, pleasure, pain and so on are stored in their appropriate places.

When some kind of memory trigger occurs, such as a question or query, the medial pre-frontal cortex sets about re-associating all the sensory strands and calling them up, to rebuild the memory. This could account for the condition where you try to recall something but have to concentrate for a few seconds before you can get a clear picture that makes sense. It sometimes takes time for the brain to find all the right pieces.

Memory Recall

Learning Ritual is predominately about memory, or more importantly, Recall.

We need to import accurate information, using whatever method ensures that the information is stored in a usable form. Then we need to be able to retrieve it, quickly, and in the right order. To do this well, we need to learn how to trust our powers of recall. The more we use recall, the stronger it will become, just like muscle training.

There are dozens of books on training your memory, but for our purposes we will use a really simple and easy technique to train and learn to trust our recall powers.

In the next section you are going to dive right in and start memorising your work, using a structure which will tell you exactly what you need to do, every day. In this Stage, the key objective is to memorise the Work, so you will be reciting parts of the Ritual, both silently and aloud, a lot.

Each time you hit a snag, your immediate temptation will be to reach for the Book. That's probably an involuntary reflex action, but it's the wrong thing to do, because it holds back your commitment to really trusting your own abilities.

So, whilst you are learning and reciting, every time you forget a word or lose your way, you should do the following;

- Place your finger to your lips
- Pause for (about) ten seconds
- Dig deep inside to retrieve the lost word or phrase

At first it will only work occasionally, but as you progress, you might be surprised at how you improve your hit-rate. As you get better at it, you won't need the whole ten seconds. If you can get better than three seconds by the end of the process, you should be able to beat your Prompter most of the time!

Co-incidentally the same gesture crops up in Royal Arch Ritual, as a trigger to 'Remember Your Obligation'.

It's very important that you use this physical 'quietener' to kick-off a recall event, which is why we use the finger to the lips because most people associate it with quietness. It's also a gesture that won't draw any attention if you do it on a bus or a train! You can substitute one of your own if you like.

Use this technique every time whilst you are learning the Ritual, so that it becomes automatic. Training your recall is mandatory if you want to master performance-level Ritual. It's easy, and it's free, so start using it right away.

Photographic Memory

Everyone's heard about people who have the fabled 'photographic memory'. It's true; some people can recall a detailed map or plan after only the briefest view. If you look for Steven Wiltshire on YouTube, you will be stunned by this autistic artist's remarkable abilities to recreate entire cityscapes after only a 45-minute aerial view.

Of course, people like Steven are rare; however it appears that most of us are blessed with some degree of visual recall ability which can be developed, and in fact will develop on its own if it's used properly.

Among the weapons in your Ritual armoury, you will, over time, subconsciously store the position of words and phrases on the pages of your Ritual book. I have found that the phrases which are particularly memorable are the ones which run across from one page to another, particularly the bottom of a left hand page to the top of a right hand page. This type of recall can be useful in remembering the sequence of paragraphs.

How Much Time?

In the previous Chapter, we discussed how to calculate the time needed to prepare your Work for performance. The example we are going to use now is the Third Principal's (Historical) Lecture, for two reasons. Firstly it is a 'pure' monologue which means it is ideal for learning on your own. Secondly it is a suitable length to be learned in a reasonable timeframe, in this case the time between successive Chapter Meetings. Thirdly, you will definitely have an opportunity to perform it at some stage in your progressions through the Offices.

Unlike some of the examples we used in the Craft Ritual (principally the Second Degree Charge) which are endued with obvious natural break-points, the Chapter Ritual, and this Lecture specifically, call for a more creative approach. Some of the paragraphs are much longer, and you will need to split them. If you are going to follow this example, now is the time to type or write the text (taking care to preserve and Secrets contained in it) and familiarise yourself with the flow of the language and figure out where your break points should occur. There are approximately 620 words in this Lecture, and I recommend your largest learning 'Section' should not be more than 40 words. Please experiment with the break points so that they will make some sense whist you are memorising them (remember, you are only trying to implant the text, not so much the meaning at this stage). You should arrive at something between 18 and 22 sections.

Again referring back to the previous book 'Learning Masonic Ritual', we allocated one day in the Cramming Stage for each section, to memorise it sufficiently to move onto the next stage of the process. In the Royal Arch Ritual, because the language will be less familiar to you, and you will not have heard it as often (nor will you, during your Chapter career) we will lengthen the time allocated for each Section to two days. So, if you have twenty sections, you will need to allocate forty days to this Cramming Phase, and using the calculation formula in the previous section (Making Your Plan) you will need a total of eighty days, around twelve weeks, to complete the Historical Lecture to performance standard. This timetable will allow you to learn thoroughly, at a relatively relaxed pace, without disruption to your daily routine. By following the system, you will be competent to perform this Lecture three months after you read it for the first time.

The key to Cramming is short bursts of focused activity, just a few minutes each day, using automated cues to trigger you to practice. The most important thing is to get cracking on it straight away. On no account should you procrastinate. You know the task, so you need to immediately put your plan in place.

Why Cramming Works Best

As we introduced earlier, this learning method requires you to memorise the complete Ritual passage as your first priority. This works because it then gives you the maximum time to polish and rehearse the whole Ceremony, so that all the parts are equally ingrained in your memory.

The alternative, which you may have tried, is to learn it sequentially, pacing out the major sections over the whole time leading up to the meeting. You may have perfected the early sections, but if your timetable slips at all, you might not get to the last few sections until you are close to the meeting date. This means you may have learned the first two thirds really well, but you're taking a huge risk because you haven't spent anywhere near as much time on the last part. You will often see the result of this method in a Lodge or Chapter, when the performance is perfect at the beginning but starts needing prompts in the last section.

So the sole objective of this first phase is to memorise the passage in rough form as quickly as possible. Of course, different people will have different capacities for memorising, and different calls on their time, but in general it would be reasonable to memorise a small paragraph every couple of days, somewhere between twenty and forty words.

Setting Up a Daily Routine

So, you have your outline plan for the first phase. How do you now ensure that each section goes in and stays in so that the parts build into a whole?

Morning Routine

For most people, their mind is most receptive and agile within the first few minutes of waking up in the morning. The best time to memorise something verbal and new is first thing in the morning, before the distractions of the normal day start to get in the way.

Of course, I don't live with you, so I don't know how your daily routine goes. It's more than likely, however, that you get some 'alone time' first thing in the morning, probably in the bathroom. This is Prime Time for Ritual learning. I strongly recommend that even if you struggle to fit your learning in during the rest of the day, you focus on this early 'session' as a priority. Have your book with you, or a copy of the section you are learning for the day, and read it through.

Silent versus Out Loud

Learning out loud is always best. It acts on more than one sensory channel in your brain, and also introduces breathing and tonality at an early stage. You should always look for opportunities to learn and rehearse out loud, though of course it might not be convenient all the time. It becomes more important in the later stages of the process, and by the time you are getting close to the Meeting you will be strongly encouraged to fully rehearse out loud at least once each day.

However, in the early stages you can practice silently as long as you focus. Even just mouthing the words as you try to memorise them will be an improvement over doing it all in your head.

Remember, you're only trying to deal with one sentence or phrase at a time, before you move on to the next one. In the next chapter, we're going to look at some tricks to help you memorise those complex little phrases that don't automatically sit well in your brain.

Take no more than ten minutes on this first exercise of the day, but try to absorb a meaningful piece of the passage, maybe a complete sentence or two. Whilst you're still holding your book, look away and see if you can recite it. If you stumble, don't immediately go back to the Book. Just place your finger to your lips, concentrate for a few seconds and see if you can recall the part you are missing. This is an important discipline to teach yourself, because if you are struggling during the rehearsal phase, or even on the day of the performance, this skill of digging down and reconstructing (recalling) the words will be very useful, and is definitely one of the Secret Weapons of a Great Ritualist.

But don't expect it to work straight away; you need to train your mind a little before you'll be able to execute 'cold recall' every time. So don't get frustrated with yourself if it takes more than a few tries before you can recite a sentence or paragraph all the way through. And especially don't worry if you're confused over the order or sequence of words in the passage; we're going to clean up the details later.

The important thing is to keep trying to recite this single short passage until you get it, just once, and it makes sense. If you've stuck to the plan so far, that should give you a little wave of satisfaction, and that's a foretaste of the bigger buzz you're going to get when you complete the whole passage in about two weeks time!

Once you've managed to recite that section once, from beginning to end, even if it's a little uncertain or out of sequence, put the book face down. This is a good time to get into the shower. Interestingly, the Ritual Book publishers have figured out that many Masons have dodgy eyesight, so they're now selling large print copies of the popular Ritual books. To date, I'm not aware of anyone publishing waterproof versions, though Freemasons being the ingenious bunch that we are, I'm fairly sure that there are Brethren and Companions who have made laminated copies of Ritual sections for the precise purpose of learning in the bath or shower!

Finding Anchors

When you are learning Ritual, you will find that some sentences and phrases are easy to retain, and some just take much longer. One technique which helps is to use the easily-memorised pieces as one type of 'anchor'. In this context, an anchor is a safe-place which allows you to periodically centre yourself in the learning process and eventually in the delivery. Once you've recognised a few anchors you will begin to have a spatial impression of the piece as a whole, and you can put your concentration into dealing with the trickier parts in-between.

As you progress, you will use larger anchors. Whole paragraphs and even whole monologues become anchors, because you can recite them on auto-pilot.

Try to find a few anchors for yourself, early in the process.

So that's the basic structure of memorising the Ritual, sentence by sentence. You will always use this method first, even when you get better at re-learning a Ceremony you've done before. You're ready for learning and memorising sequences.

To Summarise;

- Take one sentence at a time.
- Read it over again, until you are ready to try to recite it.
- If that works, keep reciting as often as you can.
- If you get stuck, place your finger to your lips and focus on trying to recall it for about 10 seconds
- If you need to, check the Book and repeat the cycle
- So let's put it into action.

Day One; Kick-Starting Your Plan

On Day One, which ideally should be the very next day after you have been allocated (or simply decided for yourself) the Work, we are setting you a very achievable target, which is the first sentence, no more than thirty words.

Follow the instructions above, and you should have it done in the first half hour of the day. If it's in the shower or the bath that you are practising, just keep going, even when you think you've learned it, until you have to do something else which requires your concentration. If you find yourself struggling with a piece of text, dig deep inside your memory and try to recall it. Don't let yourself get frustrated, just follow the sequence. If you absolutely cannot recall it, check the Book again. Alternate as many times as you need, but by the time you unlock the bathroom door, you should have most of it in place. Now go and get your breakfast!

Make Appointments with Yourself

It's up to you if you keep silently rehearsing it. If you're alone, that might be perfectly OK. But if you aren't, it might to be challenging for you, so simply drop it from your front-of-mind.

Don't worry, that short burst of intense focus and activity has set up a chain reaction in your subconscious, and the process will continue in the background without you having to focus on it. Just get on with your normal day, but before you forget, book yourself an Appointment.

Set yourself a short time-slot to revisit your learning at a convenient time of the day when you can guarantee you will not be distracted. Maybe you're going to drive to work, which is ideal because you can practice out loud if you're alone in the car. Or maybe you're catching the bus or train. It doesn't matter; just tell yourself that at a certain time, in a certain situation "I am going to check myself".

The best way to enforce this timetable is to use your mobile phone's Alarm function. Try putting some silent alarms in your phone so you don't forget to keep the appointments. It's that simple and you really don't need much time, but make sure you repeat it two or three times a day in the beginning.

If you have a Smart Phone you can set multiple alarms which will repeat at the same time every day. You can usually tag each alarm you set, so you can add a reminder of what you need to do. When the alarm triggers, it will put a notification reminder on your screen.

You can write quite long tags, so you can be quite detailed with your reminders. Once you set up the alarms, your practice timetable is on auto-pilot. This is a really powerful but very simple tool that anyone can do with very little effort.

Maybe you are going to be really busy and distracted until lunch-time, so set up your appointment accordingly. You're only going to need about three or four minutes to check yourself, but the important thing is that you stick to the timing. If you miss it, or forget, just set up another appointment as soon as you remember, and so on. The objective here is to check yourself regularly during the course of the day, so that by the time you get home in the evening (or wherever you end up) you have correctly memorised the passage of that day.

Be prepared, you may find yourself perfectly able to recite the piece at lunch-time but you've completely forgotten it by tea-time! This is normal, it happens to the best of us, and it is nothing to worry about. You haven't actually forgotten anything. You've just caught yourself out by trying to access something from a part of your memory that it has not yet penetrated, but the piece is in your mental 'system'. Check your book. Of course, you knew it all along; don't beat yourself up over it, it's all going to fall into place if you just stick to the system!

Try to fit in at least three of these little 'appointments' during the day. The number of appointments you can achieve each day will have a directly proportional effect on the speed at which you memorise the Work.

A good time to do your last 'daylight check' is just before you get home. Because for most people, once you cross the threshold from work-mode to home-mode, there's a whole new set of demands on your time, probably from your family, and they come first. So, if your final check was OK, you can shelve your learning until later.

Relax and let your mind do the hard work in the background.

Don't Try To Learn In the Evening

I purposely don't advocate setting aside time in the evening (so called 'me time') to learn Ritual. Sure, it works for some people, but it seems to fail for most people, and it never worked for me. That's not to say that evenings are off-limits, but it's 'free study' time if you like. There's no evening homework.

In the evening, especially after a day at work, tiredness and concentration are a major factor. In addition, there are numerous distractions in most people's environments in the evening, such as kids, dinner, TV, visitors, and other family responsibilities. Besides, if you follow this system, you shouldn't actually need to 'set time aside' because this method of learning is designed to fit into your everyday routine without disruption.

Having a Drink?

I'd be a hypocrite if I tried to persuade you to change any of your personal habits in the name of learning Masonic Ritual. This learning system is specifically designed to fit around your everyday life, not to force you to change your habits; after all, it's just a hobby. Nobody's going to die if you get it wrong, and you're not going to get paid if you get it right, so relax.

However, remember this; although it is perfectly possible to rehearse, repeat and recite *learned* information after a few drinks, it is extremely difficult to learn and retain *new* information. That's one of the reasons why learning the new stuff is so much more effective in the morning. If you like a drink or two in the evening, it shouldn't really impact on your Ritual learning, provided you continue to follow the rest of the system.

Evenings Are For Relaxing

To repeat, there's no obligation for you to think about the Work during the evening, as long as you stick to the morning, daytime and night time routines.

But there's nothing to stop you practising in the evening either. Everyone needs to go to the bathroom from time to time, so there are probably two or three little down-time opportunities for you to mentally or verbally recite pieces of your work. The evening is a good time to separate out any particularly troubling sentences or 'lists' that need extra repetition to remember and repeat.

Some years ago, when I was first learning about Hypnosis, I spent a week at a seminar with Paul McKenna, the famous TV hypnotist, and Richard Bandler, the founder of NLP (Neuro-Linguistic Programming). During one of the workshops I asked Paul McKenna 'do' hypnosis on me to make me leave my living room every time Eastenders came on TV, and do something more useful. In a matter of seconds the change was made, and that effect still works every time after nearly ten years!

This demonstrates the power of triggers or cues, as auto-suggestions to take some action. At the beginning it is worth setting your own cue, something like my Eastenders theme tune, to designate time when you could be doing something more useful, like practising your Ritual! It's just a small commitment you make, which is easy to stick to because it makes total sense. If you make sure you follow your cue a few times, it will quickly become a habit, with the added incentive that you too will be doing something much more useful.

Again, as long as you follow the core tasks in the system, which is to rehearse small things regularly throughout the day, you'll be in good shape by the time you get to bed-time.

Bed-Time Rehearsal

It's often been said that Masonic Ritual is a great cure for insomnia, and I can personally testify to the truth of that statement. It's right up there with Counting Sheep!

Just as the first half-hour of the day is the best time to implant new information, so is the last half-hour the ideal time to cement and solidify the 'Day's Work'. This is a major pillar in your learning system so it's important that you commit to it early.

Try this sequence, which is specifically designed so that you can fit it in with your normal night-time routine, also involving another visit to the bathroom.

First, check your learning for the day. This could be while you are brushing your teeth, since this largely precludes you from talking to anyone! Just make sure that you have memorised what you planned to learn at least 90% accurately, for that day. The same rules apply; if you are struggling, go down inside and try to use your memory recall to reconstruct the missing parts. If that fails, check the Book. The objective here is to be clear, by the time you turn out the lights, so that the last thing you do before you sleep is to mentally recite your Ritual piece.

This is the perfect time for solidifying and confirming learned information. As you descend into the dreamy somnambulist state just before sleep, you are mimicking self-hypnosis, which is an ideal state for learning. Just lie there and practice your words, in your head. In the dark, without distraction, you will be able to find a focus and concentration which is often difficult to achieve during the day, so this is a very valuable time for the Ritualist.

People sometimes say "but I have so much on my mind". Well, you'll have to switch your priorities for a few minutes. Sorry, but even with this system, there is some sacrifice required!

Right from the early days of learning a passage, as you build the pieces, sentence by sentence and phrase by phrase, you'll probably find that the tranquillising effect will have you sleeping like a baby before you get to the end. And the additional benefit is that there is (according to some branches of sleep science) a remanence effect in the brain which will keep on processing your last thoughts for a short period after you nod off. I cannot attest to the veracity of such claims, but I can tell you that it works well for me and I have reports from many others that it works for them too.

Whatever the case, that final few minutes of silent mental repetition should complete your day's learning and set you up nicely for…

Day Two and Beyond

So, you wake up on the morning of Day 2.

We already established a system for you to learn the day's

passage, but first you need to check that yesterday's piece is still in there, which it should be. If it's vague, you have the tools at your disposal; first try memory recall. If that doesn't work, check the Book. Practice yesterday's piece a few times, just to connect the dots in your memory again. Assuming you are now comfortable, which if you have followed the system so far you will be, and we're ready to move on.

Previously, we established that the added complexity of Royal Arch Ritual may dictate that you use two days to learn each short section, rather than the one day method we employed for the more familiar Craft Ritual. This will of course vary from person to person. If you have based your timetable on two-days-per-section, then you'll use every second day to cement and solidify what you learned the day before, in advance of moving on to the next section.

It's important that you feel comfortable and in control of each section before you move onto the next one. If you can achieve that in one-day-per-section, then move ahead more quickly. Otherwise, stick to the two-day convention, and on alternate days just work through the previous day's learning until you have it thoroughly ingrained in your memory. You have enough time.

There's nothing different about the way you're going to memorise the next sentence or paragraph. What is most important is to learn it as a standalone piece.

Just do exactly the same as before, read it through as many times as it takes to be able to start to recite it, then check, re-check, recall, and eventually put the book down and jump in the shower. What worked for you yesterday is going to work for you today, just the same, so you can be confident that you are well on the way to memorising the whole Ceremony.

But there's a difference today; once you have a basic grasp of this second piece of Work (and remember we're not concerned with detail at this stage) you can, when you're ready, put the two pieces together.

Now, this might frustrate you a little for the first few tries, but persevere. Remember; you KNOW the Work from yesterday. What may happen is that, just when you think you've got a handle on today's work, you try to out the two pieces together and although you can easily repeat section one, the new stuff just evaporates when you get to it. That's no problem. Again, use your memory recall, because it's in there somewhere and you just need to find it. Check the Book as a final resort whenever you get really stuck, but put it down each time and force yourself to dig deep in your memory.

Your objective before you start your day properly is to be able to recite the two pieces together, with 90% accuracy.

As with Day One, you need to make those little appointments with yourself, so set the alarms on your phone and that will jog you into your learning zone without you having to make a decision. It works, so please use it. The more we can automate the process, the more effective it will be.

We talked before about your evening routine, which probably varies a lot from day-to-day, but you'll now have a good idea about your own capabilities, so you can tune your rehearsal schedule up or down to accommodate yourself. The key milestones are the mornings. You shouldn't move on until you're 90% solid on the previous day's Work.

Occasionally, you may miss a milestone and you won't be ready to move on to the next passage, so don't. Just add another day to yesterday's Work and make sure you've got it. You have a couple of extra days built into your schedule, but please try to keep up with your original plan as far as possible. There's no such thing as too much rehearsal time, as you'll learn in the later Stages...

Follow the pattern as closely as possible for each section; that is

First 30 Minutes;

- Quick revision of yesterday's learning, checking that it's still there and checking the book to bring it back. Put it aside

- Start working on the next section, following the same memorisation technique

- When you're ready, try all the sections together.

- Set up your micro-alarms for your three daytime rehearsal slots.

- Do your last 'daylight check' before you settle into your evening activity.

- Take little opportunities to recite the work during the evening, if you can.

- At bed-time, check yourself before lights out, and then rehearse in your mind whilst you fall asleep.

Onwards and Upwards

Within a few days you should be getting the hang of this method and feel it working for you. The most important thing about this first stage is to stay focussed on cramming the memorising process, so that you quickly assemble the complete passage, building sentence by sentence. To repeat, we are not so concerned about the detail, the little link words, or even the order of word sequence at this early stage. What is most important is to get the sentences and paragraphs in the correct order.

Once you are two or three days in, you have proven to yourself that you have the intellectual faculties to learn this kind of prose, so you should have no lack of confidence going forwards. It becomes a mechanical process which you can re-use every time you learn.

Of course as you gradually build up the passage, your rehearsal time will expand. But this is not a problem. The complete Historical Lecture takes less than four minutes to deliver, so finding a few time slots throughout the day should present no problem for most people.

Splitting the Sections

As I mentioned earlier you'll regularly see Ceremonies which start out brilliantly but deteriorate towards the end. This is usually because the person has used a purely linear structure for their learning. They may have rehearsed the first half of the Ceremony for several weeks, but the last part only got a few days at the end.

Whilst you're in this memorisation phase, you shouldn't try to manage sections of Ritual more than one page in length at a time. So, in the example of this Historical Lecture, that's a simple three-way division as there are three clear sections (The First, Second and Third Lodges) which are each approximately one page in length..

Once you've done the first section (The First Lodge),

you're going to mentally box it off, and treat the second section of the Ceremony as an entirely separate piece. This breakdown gives you a big advantage when you're learning, and also adds an additional memory aid into your toolbox for later.

We're certainly not going to discard the first section, because if you don't tend to it, it will start to decay. The first section will be the first thing you mentally rehearse when you wake up in the morning, and the first thing you mentally recite when you put the lights out at bed time. You will keep working it, ensuring that it becomes more and more natural to you. But you won't try to join it up with the second and third sections until you have finished memorising those separately.

These 'Page Breaks' will ensure that you give equal focus and attention to each section of the Ceremony, so that when you do finally connect the three parts, you know them more or less equally. Then the entire rehearsal phase will be balanced, and this will be repeated in your performance.

If you make a checklist as shown in the previous chapter for your Work, by marking each time you run through a section in the daily boxes, you can easily see which parts are being neglected, so that you give every section equal attention through the week.

This break-down approach will work fine for all Chapter Ritual; however we will look at some modifications when we discuss the PS Work at Exaltation, the key important Ceremony which you will need to master on your way through the Chapter Offices.

Down-Time Opportunities

Most people have lots of small opportunities to do a little Ritual practice. How many of these would work for you?

- In the bathroom
- Walking to the bus stop or rail station
- Waiting for the bus or train
- On the bus, on the train
- Instead of reading a magazine
- Eating your breakfast or lunch
- In a queue

- Driving the car
- Doctor's waiting room
- The Dentist Chair (this one is brilliant)
- In a taxi
- Walking somewhere,
- Exercising in the gym
- Cycling or Jogging
- Walking the dog
- Washing the car

To master the memorisation phase, you'll need to commit yourself to at least a few of these opportunities. Think about it in terms of using dead time for something useful, and it will start to deliver big benefits as you work your way through the initial memorisation or cramming phase.

The Sum of the Parts

In our example, The Historical Lecture, you broke down the Ritual into short sentences or paragraphs and learned them one by one. In addition, you broke down the whole passage into three one-page sections. If you have done those correctly, followed the system, and stuck to your timetable and milestones, you should have all the parts committed to memory in around six weeks, or maybe even faster.

Now it's time to put the three sections together, and try your first full-length run through.

Remember we're not looking for perfection yet. But when you put it all together for the first time it should begin to make some kind of logical sense. As we said at the beginning, the Lecture is basically a presentation of historical facts to the Candidate. You may perhaps continue to remember the sequence because you used a numbering system from the start, which is fine. Alternately, you may have memorised each sentence in terms of how it follows on from the one before it.

However you have done it, Congratulations. That's the hardest part. You've assembled the ingredients. Soon we'll start to focus on Stage Two, when you'll perfect and polish the language, and cook the whole dish.

The next Chapter will deal with some more detailed techniques that will help you begin to interpret the language that you have memorised, and start getting it ready for serious Rehearsal

Cheat Sheet

The Historical Lecture explains the origins of the Three Lodges which underpin regular Freemasonry. When you learn and deliver this lecture, you'll be looking for cues, anchors and triggers which help you to get everything in the correct sequence.

Of course, the sequence 'First, Second, Third' is the most obvious one. If you also focus on quickly memorising the place where each Lodge was founded, and the people who officiated, you will have a really good set of anchors to carry you through the performance.

The Historical Lecture has its own, perfectly legitimate 'Cheat Sheet' which you can use as a learning aid whilst you memorise the sequence.

If you have served in the office of PS, you will be familiar with the Questions Before The Toasts, which are asked at the Festive Board by the MEZ and answered by the PS. This small Ceremony is written towards the back of your Ritual Book, and is actually a cut-down version of the Historical Lecture. You can use it, either because you already learned and memorised it, or simply by having it open when you are practising going through the full-scale Lecture, to jog your memory about the key features and characters of each section of the lecture.

Summary

- The Objective is to Cram or Memorize the Work to 90% accuracy, as quickly as possible.

- Set up your Morning Routine as the best time to start the new Work for the day.

- Focus on using Memory Recall before you reach for the Book.

- Set up a Daily Practice Routine, using Alarms on your phone.

- Recite Out Loud whenever possible, for maximum benefit.

- Relax in the Evening, but do a little practice whenever

you get an opportunity

- Set up Cues and Triggers to 'do something useful'.

- Use Bed-Time as the best time to silently rehearse.

- Break the whole Work into page-size sections so you learn each section equally.

- Use a paper 'Checklist' to plot your progress and balance your efforts.

- Find small 'down-time' opportunities to fit in a little practice.

- Remember; the more you do, the quicker you'll complete Stage One.

Chapter 5
Polishing & Refining

Stage Two – Polishing & Refining

Now that you have completed the Cramming stage, you should be able to recite the whole Ceremony from start to finish, even if you're not completely verbatim. The objective of Stage One was to get the language into your memory by whatever means possible, so that you have the raw material to start to build your eventual performance.

In this second Stage, you are going to take what you have and work on the detail. The key objective now is to nurture the Ceremony or Lecture, and achieve the following;

- Finally memorise an authentic version, ideally the same as the Book.
- Incorporate rhythm, anchors, cues and lists, so that it becomes natural to you.
- Practice constantly, until the recital becomes technically automatic and you no longer have to think about the words you are saying.
- Use different techniques to check yourself and build your confidence.

Filling In the Detail

As we have seen, it's not so important to nail the details right at the beginning. If you watch a landscape painter, he starts with a rough sketch of the proportions, and then progressively loads in detail, section by section, until the final piece is ready. If you could only see the picture, and not the scene he is painting, you would not recognise anything significant until the final stage.

Let's assume that you have completed the rough memorisation of your Work, or maybe our example Historical Lecture in around five weeks. Now we enter a new phase, which is to refine the language so that it synchronises with the Book. Of course it would be great to be word-perfect by the time you get to your Chapter Meeting, but most Ritual doesn't achieve that perfection, and most Companions don't expect it, so we will concentrate as usual on practical methods to get you to an acceptable standard.

In this phase of the process, there are numerous techniques you can employ to help you. Once again, we put a time limit on ourselves, because it's important to get to the final Rehearsal stage with plenty of time to spare. You will recall the timetable formula in an earlier section. Stage 2 (Polishing) should be allocated half the time of Stage 1 (Cramming).

This chapter is really about checking what you have memorised, and correcting the language. At this point in the process, let's make the assumption that you have understood both the language and the general meaning of the Ritual you are learning. By now, if there are any abbreviations or terms which are unclear to you, you should have asked someone for an explanation.

Maintaining Your Practice Routines

Earlier in the process, you were shown how to set-up specific routines to ensure you made small time-investments in the Ritual every day. Ideally you are using the Alarm function on your phone to remind you when it's time to do a few minutes Work. By now this structure should be working well for you. It shows that if you apply some direct focus for a few minutes every few hours, you create a subconscious momentum which keeps working in the background. Each time you come to check up on yourself, you've moved forwards without really consciously trying.

For this stage, it's ideal if you can maintain the same 'slots' each day. However, you need to use the time in different ways, so you might need to re-organise your Ritual schedule a little bit.

Hands-Free versus Hands-On

Some of the time, you can be 'Hands Free' which means you are simply reciting your Work, without necessarily referring to the Book or any other copy of the Ritual. This is pure practice time, and it's really important, because now you are close to having an authentic version of the Work at your fingertips. You're using spaced repetition to improve your familiarity with the piece, which will help with your confidence in the final Stage.

At other times you will need to be more 'Hands On', using some of the following techniques to audit and check your progress, and create additional learning tools for yourself.

It's important to keep your morning 'Bathroom Routine' going. You'll recall that we identified first thing in the day as the optimum time to learn new information. It's also a good time to revise what you did the day before. In the early morning, your brain is at full power and you aren't pre-occupied by the accumulating distractions that build up during the course of a normal day.

Your morning routine in Stage 2 is a simple recital session, either silently or, if you can do it, out loud. Whilst you go through your routine, just make little mental notes of any places where you're still unsure of what you are reciting. If you like, you can put pencil marks in your Ritual Book, and then erase them as you fix each variance.

Your bed-time routine is completely 'Hands Free'. If you've been following this structure for your memorisation phase, you should be getting the benefits from this session, both in terms of cementing the Ritual into your memory, and helping you to get off to sleep! So keep going with that last mental recital each night.

The most important thing in this Polishing phase is that you actually notice that you are eliminating errors and glitches each morning and evening. Accuracy and fluency are the key attributes you are aiming to develop in this Stage.

Hands-On Polishing

Next, you'll read about some practical tools and techniques that you can use to really boost your accuracy and familiarity with the Work. These require a little bit more effort, so you need to be able to find some hands-on time. If you can manage thirty minutes every other day, you should be able to master your Work within the time allotted for this Stage.

Remember, this section is targeting accuracy and precision, and really is all about repetition. Each time you go through your Work without relying on a printed or recorded copy, you are embedding it deeper and deeper into your learned memory bank. You might not fully appreciate this the first time you learn it, but it will be much simpler when you get a chance to use it for the second time.

A Word about Boredom

Learning Ritual can get boring occasionally. It starts out challenging, but after you have repeated the same piece of language a few dozen times (or even a few hundred times, when you move on to the bigger passages) you may start to feel a bit fed up with it.

Understand that boredom is a positive outcome at this stage. It implies that you've successfully memorised your Work, and that remembering and reciting has ceased to trouble or even challenge you. So turn it to your advantage. When you feel too bored to do your two or three minutes of rehearsal, push yourself to try for a 'perfect recital' in order to prove to yourself how brilliant you are. Then, instead of feeling bored and guilty that you skipped a session, you can feel smug and cocky that you did it with one hand tied behind your back!

Whatever you do, don't succumb to the boredom and be tempted to stop or slow down. It's a temporary thing, which will pass. The trick is to have a clear vision of the target you are shooting for, which is to give a good performance in the Chapter. That will definitely not be boring!

So, maintain the momentum by sticking to your daily routine, something like;

- Morning (bathroom) routine; Up to ten minutes full recital (that's long enough for at least one full Historical Lecture, or one of the three major sections of the PS Exaltation Ceremony) without the Book
- Morning Commute; Silent recital on public transport, checking yourself after each section. Alternately, recital out-loud if you're alone in the car.
- Lunch-Time; try to fit in a read-through or some type-checking if you can. Every couple of days is enough, as long as you focus.
- Final 'Daylight Check'; review any 'upgrades'; you've made that day, making sure you have definitely incorporated them into your mental 'Master Copy'
- Take the evening off. There are more important things than Chapter. (Unless it's Chapter of Improvement)
- Bed-Time; Your final run-through of the day. A good time to start visualising the actual Ceremony, particularly mentally practising the perambulations if you need to.

The Techniques in Stage Two

Sequences of Words (Lists)

Many Ritual passages have 'lists' inside, such as the Five Noble Orders Of Architecture, The Seven Liberal Arts and Sciences, the Four Cardinal Virtues and so on. Some people have the kind of memory which enables them to memorise these short sequences easily, others do not. Learning lists is just another technique, and if you separate these tricky sequences out, you can learn them much more easily. When you perform the Ritual, confident recital of the 'lists' are important. They form anchors to the whole piece.

These sequences are also important because many Companions in the Chapter, whilst having forgotten or never learned the Ritual you are performing, will have unconsciously memorised these sequences as a result of having been in the audience many times. So it's important not only to get the words correct, but also to get them in the correct order. Everyone will be mentally prompting you!

So if you have ever struggled with these sequences, it's a good idea to separate them out and learn them as standalone items, and the ideal time to do this is in the middle of Stage Two.

In the current example, the Historical Lecture, here are the Lists;

- The First or Holy Lodge
- The Second or Sacred Lodge
- The Third or Grand and Royal Lodge

and

- Moses, Aholiab, and Bezaleel
- S, K of I - H, K of T & HAB
- Z, Prince of the People, H, the prophet, and J, the son of Josedech the High Priest

and

- The Foot of Mount Horeb in the Wilderness of Sinai
- in the bosom of the Holy Mount Moriah
- at Jerusalem

There are some tips and tricks for using abbreviations and other memory cues later on, but for now it is sufficient to point out that these sequences can easily be separated out and learned in isolation, after which they will re-integrate back into your learning quite smoothly.

Visualisation

Visualisation can be a useful tool if you are mentally rehearsing Officers Work involving perambulations, particularly for the PS. It's also handy to practise the Opening and Closing Ceremonies for the Principals.

Some people recommend you use visualisation to learn the spoken Ritual itself. I'm on the fence about this: I understand and appreciate the value of visualisation because it is used to great effect in Sports Psychology, Hypnotherapy, and even Guided Meditation. I previously suggested it as a technique that can be used in very small and focused doses in the Memorisation or Cramming Phase.

But in terms of a learning aid for Ritual text, for many people it just adds an extra unwanted step.

In his book 'Ritual in Mind', Graham Chisnell lays out a memory system for Learning Masonic Ritual Tools using Visualisation as its central plank, should you feel inclined to explore this method for yourself.

'List' Learning Tips and Tricks

- Learn Lists separately, and then integrate them into the main passage.
- Find acronyms to jog your memory.

- Learn your Lists early. Use them as anchor points and links when you learn the passage.

Acronyms are a great way to remember lists. Visualisation is a valid technique for some people. Numbered lists work for others. The most important thing is to learn lists separately to the passage, and use your 'list competence' as an anchor point in the whole Ceremony.

Link Words

In listening to Ritual in many Lodges and Chapters, what come up time and again are errors related to the almost inconsequential small words which link all the big words together. Tenses, genders and so on are often overlooked in learning Ritual, usually because the Companion concerned has not allowed himself enough time in this middle 'Polishing' phase.

The easiest way to approach this is by a gradual process of correction. Once you have the rough passage committed to memory, it is much simpler to read through it in the Book and you will easily notice the places where you may be using an incorrect word or phrase. It's then a simple matter to recite that part of the Ritual and check that you are now using the right word (for example an 'and' instead of an 'or'). You will then find in most cases that the next time you run through the full passage, you'll mentally remind yourself to use the new correct word when you reach that point. After two or three run-throughs, the new word or words are seamlessly integrated into your mental 'Master Copy' of the passage.

To summarise this simple technique;

- Recite a good-sized portion of your Work

- Read through it again (out loud) from the Book
- Your errors will be usually be obvious
- Run over those sentences three or four times
- Recite the passage again
- If necessary, rinse and repeat!

Again, we're not looking for absolute perfection, because there are other techniques that will help to clean up any remaining errors. However, you should aim to be better than 95% accurate before you move on.

For the more ambitious Ritualist, this is a useful skill to master in case you find yourself switching between two different Ritual conventions (for example Domatic and Aldersgate) if you are a guest in another Chapter. The little variances make a big difference, especially to the audience.

Acronyms and Abbreviations

When you come across a small phrase that troubles your memory, it is a useful trick to replace it mentally with an acronym which means something to you personally, even if you make it up, and which is then much simpler to recall and position in sequence. Hence 'Moses, Aholiab and Bezaleel' simply becomes M.A.B. and it may help you to apply this kind of acronym as a memory aid.

Going one stage further, some acronyms are easier to remember if you substitute other words, which may be familiar terms to you.

Many competent Ritualists I have met use this technique, but like all the other tips and tricks in this book, you need to find the ones that work for you. If you'd like to try the Acronym method for yourself, there's a really good web resource at **www.acronymfinder.com**

Testing Yourself

By now, you should be achieving about 95% accuracy and you should not be hitting any road-blocks when you recite the whole Ceremony. Next you will spend a little time immersed in checking your precision, which will enable you to clear up any outstanding glitches.

So, let's go back to the beginning. Carrying the Book and reading it on the bus might be one way of getting you there, but it's probably not the best way. We need a more sophisticated approach.

Marking Your Ritual Book

Your Ritual Book is part of your Masonic time capsule. It was probably given to you by your Proposer into Craft or Chapter, and it may have sentimental or nostalgic value for you. It's only a Book, and there are thousands like it, but this particular copy may be special to you. If you would prefer to preserve it unsullied, you should.

I which case I suggest you buy another one, as your 'Working Book'. You can mark-up parts of the Work, maybe by underlining passages, or even in different highlight colours to help you learn and re-learn them each time you need to. When I was PS, I found it really helpful to highlight all my own words and perambulations in my Working Book so that I could skip through the whole Ceremony and just concentrate on my parts, by quickly identifying the cues for me to begin and end.

I really recommend you do this, and also annotate other parts where you find it useful to be able to directly draw your attention without wading through pages that aren't relevant to you. It will save you lots of time and effort, which is key to this learning method.

Typing

First a general word about typing and the Work. If you are a competent typist and are happy using the word processing program on a PC or Mac, this can act as a very substantial asset when learning Work.

The Rulers of the Craft are unspecific on the legitimacy of typing the Work. Of course the Entrusting Obligation in your Exaltation Ceremony exhorts you conceal the secrets imparted to you and keep inviolate the mystic rites. Received wisdom is that the Secrets are, in conventional Working, any words, names or phrases which are abbreviated or blanked out in the Ritual Book. For the purpose of the learning process as described in this Book, I subscribe to that convention. This is logical, I think you'd agree, since any ordinary member of the public can walk into a regalia shop and buy a Ritual Book off-the-shelf without any need to identify themselves as a Freemason. Likewise, most of the Ceremonies can be easily found on the Internet, and often such postings do not even conform to the convention of protecting the Secrets.

Copyright

Of course there is the Law of Copyright, which is there to protect the owner of the printed material from people ripping it off and illegitimately profiting from it. As an author myself, I am wholly supportive of this important law, because without it the entire creative community (writers, artists, musicians, and so on) would starve! The law is clear: you cannot copy protected Work, and that includes both written and recorded copying.

However, there is a facility in copyright law called "Fair Use", which allows for the limited use of copies for specific non-commercial applications. According to the Copyright Service in the UK, this allows for "research and private study" without infringing copyright.

A mainstream example is the use of textbooks in schools, where it is quite normal for students to write or type verbatim passages in their course Work. You might reasonably interpret this as allowing you to re-type a passage of Ritual and use it for your own private study, as long as you do not make it available to anyone else, by any means. I would also suggest that this practice would only be reasonable provided that you had purchased a legitimate version of the original Work in the first place, i.e. you bought a Ritual Book, so that the author and publisher have lost nothing in the process.

If you are in any doubt about your rights and responsibilities regarding copyright, I would refer you to **www.copyrightservice.co.uk**, the authority site on such matters in the UK.

It is reasonable to conclude therefore that it's okay to type the Work as long as you buy the Book, don't type the Secrets and don't share it with anyone else (they can do it for themselves!)

Typing Ritual has a multiplying effect on the learning process, because it forces you to read and interpret, and to memorise for the short-term. There's a strong communications channel between your eyes and your hands, and information passes through several processes between you reading it to actually pressing the right keys to type it out. You will certainly be using your memory to store the little pieces of information whilst you put them through the various stages of conversion from a visual image to a set of complex actions, and these small memories are absorbed into your overall knowledge of the piece.

Next, as you type there is a further inception process going on in your brain. This time your eyes are reading, and your brain is auditing the correctness of your typing, so again you are interpreting the image and giving it a 'pass/fail' check against your original memory.

Typing into a PC also gives you numerous advantages in terms of the portability and versatility of the 'script'. Once you have an electronic version, you can do other things with it to help you learn, as long as you stay within the copyright law. Obviously you can print out sections of the Ritual on small pages and carry them in your pocket or in your wallet, which gives you multiple opportunities to check the Work whilst you are learning it, without having to carry a Ritual Book with you.

Additionally, most word processing software allows you to store documents in different formats, different page sizes, and different font sizes. One of the most useful facilities, to be found in virtually all modern word processing programs, is the ability to store a document as a 'portable document format' PDF file, which can then be read in Adobe Acrobat as well as a host of other third-party programs. The greatest advantage of PDF files is that they can be side-loaded onto smart phones, tablets, and E-readers such as the Amazon Kindle. So now you have your Ritual Book on virtually any device. PDF files on your smart phone enable you to learn Ritual passages on the bus or the train without it looking as though you're on your way to a Bible class!

At the time of writing, most of the major Ritual Societies and publishers have not made the 'Books' available on the Kindle store. Sales of electronic Books are now overhauling physical printed copies in many categories, and the Ritual Book would seem to lend itself perfectly to such treatment!

If you decide to use this method, there are a few things that are worth knowing which will save you some time. First of all, when you are typing into your PC it's best to use a small page size setup, such as A6. It's more suitable for the size of the screen that you are going to be using. Secondly, choose a font size which is going to be readable on your smart-phone: A minimum 14 or 16 point size is fine, and you should try to use a serifated font such as Times New Roman, which is generally easier to read in blocks of text.

Finally, set up the margins as 'narrow', and this will, in conjunction with the other two points, give you a wholly readable display on the phone screen.

If it is not your intention to use a tablet, Kindle, or smart phone in this way, it is still useful to set up your typed document so that, for example, you create four "panels" of text on an A4 printed sheet, so that you can fold it into quarters which will slip neatly into your wallet or pocket. Use the 'columns' function and move the paragraphs around until you get a nice position for the folds in the paper.

Comparison Checking

Another useful tool when re-typing the Ritual is that you can self-check your understanding and memorisation. Many Word Processing apps give you the ability to Compare Documents side-by-side, a practice often used by lawyers when checking contracts (known as Legal Blackline). To do this, you will first need to create a "Master" document, which is a correct facsimile of the Ritual you are learning. Put that aside, and when you are ready to practice your recital, create a new blank document and re-type the passage from memory. Once you have done this you can use the "Compare Documents" function in Word which will show you the variations (i.e. your mistakes) inside the master document.

If you have followed the recommendations earlier in the Book, particularly in terms of cramming the "big-picture" early in the process, then this method will help you to refine your precision, and if you repeat it regularly you will clearly see the progress you are making in eliminating grammatical errors and syntax mistakes.

Nobody expects you to be perfect, however there's nothing stopping you from trying!

An excellent Application for smart phones and tablets is PDF Reader, which costs £1.99 on the Apple App Store at time of writing. It has some great features, such as the ability to receive documents as e-mails and then store them in custom folders on your phone or tablet. Indeed, Adobe themselves now have an Adobe Reader Application which can be downloaded for free on both Apple and Android devices.

So, What If You Don't Type?

All of the above methods Work perfectly well with handwriting, but of course it is difficult to carry handwriting onto an electronic device. Nevertheless, writing and re-writing the Ritual longhand is a perfectly valid method of memorising the Work.

Index cards or Post-It notes can do the job if you prefer handwriting.

The Naughty Schoolboy Method

When I was a lad….

I don't know if they still enforce this kind of punishment in school, but when I was a boy, a well-known and hated penalty for misbehaviour was the "100 Lines". I'm sure you know about this, because it's such a cliché, but in case you don't, it goes like this;

If you were caught (for example) copying someone else's schoolwork, you might be ordered by your teacher to "write a hundred lines". The line would typically be something like…

"I must not copy other people's Work"

…which you would be compelled to write long-hand, usually during a detention period, then present to the teacher and your punishment would be discharged. In the case of particularly vindictive teachers, or particularly heinous offences, the lines might have to be written in chalk on the blackboard (another historical curiosity). Whatever the case, a by-product of the punishment was that the particular sentence, after a hundred repetitions, was so well ingrained into your consciousness (and subconsciousness) that it would stay there for a long, long time. Whether it actually had any beneficial effect on your dreadful behaviour is debatable!

It is definitely low-tech, but the same principle can be used to learn particularly troublesome short passages, and quickly.

I first experimented with this the first time I tried to learn the Royal Arch Mystical Lecture, which you may have heard. The whole lecture is quite complicated, but there is a particularly irksome paragraph concerning 'The Name on the Circle' which is horrible to memorize. Having struggled with it for days, I broke it down into its five natural sections, each a long sentence, and over a period of five days I used the 'writing lines' method in order to memorise each sequence of words. I discovered that the optimum exercise was to write each line twenty times, and to repeat the exercise three times a day, first thing in the morning, sometime in the afternoon, and once in the evening just before bed. It's about five minutes each time, and it's a great excuse to buy one of those elegant Moleskine notebooks that people from Advertising Agencies carry around.

The beauty of the Naughty Schoolboy method, which is, I repeat, only really practical for those particularly troublesome short passages, is that you don't actually have to tax your memory at all. You can copy the first line directly from the Book if you want, and then copy each subsequent line from the one above. All you do is spend a few minutes copying and writing, and your marvellous subconscious memory does the rest for you.

It really works! In terms of how and where you might apply it when learning our example, the Historical Lecture, by this mid-point in the learning process you will have already identified some passages which may be causing you some angst, and this is a good technique to employ in order to get quickly past these troublesome obstacles.

Rhythm and Metering

Whatever its origins, there's no doubt that the Royal Arch Ritual is exquisitely constructed, and packed full of patterns and rhythms which, if you train yourself to recognise them, can be very useful in helping you to memorise and perform the Ceremonies well. It would also be true to say that some of the language is arguably clumsy and does not flow at all well, but there are highlights throughout every Ceremony which, if you identify and learn them properly, can be used as 'anchors', those safe landing points which are spaced throughout the Ceremonies as places of familiarity and comfort.

A really good example of rhythmic Ritual, almost a song in itself, is this passage from the PS Exaltation Ceremony, in the 'Three MM's from Babylon' section;

> We would scorn to be descended
> From those who basely fled
> When the city and Holy Temple
> Were sorely oppressed

If that doesn't speak to you at first, try tapping your foot along to an imaginary beat whilst you read it out loud, and you'll soon get it. Imagine each line is a musical bar, and has two beats

The Chapter Ritual is full of examples of rhythm and metering that you'll find can be applied to help with learning. It's not a magic bullet, but it is another tool which you can add to your box of tricks that make it easier to remember those tricky passages.

When you first read a Ritual passage aloud to yourself, you might immediately start to spot these little 'rhythm sections'. You can mark them with a highlight pen as you discover them, and they may quickly become the parts you learn first that hang the whole thing together for you.

Starting To Rehearse

In this Chapter we have cemented some techniques to get you through Stage Two by focusing on memorising, checking and reciting the authentic version of the Work you're learning. Now we need to think about transitioning to Stage Three, the Rehearsal phase. It's important that you confirm to yourself that the Work is now solidly implanted into your memory.

You can't really start rehearsing the delivery until you've mastered the text. If you have followed the instructions so far, you should be well on the way to that by now.

Summary

- In Stage Two, the objective is to Polish your Work until it is accurate and automatic
- Maintain your Practice Schedule using the same Alarm techniques as Stage One
- The Morning and Bed-Time routines are very valuable
- Identify Lists and Sequences and learn them separately
- Practice Visualisation to help with Perambulations.
- Use repetition to identify and correct small 'link word' errors.
- Use familiar acronyms and abbreviations to remember tricky phrases
- Mark-up your Ritual Book. Buy a second one if necessary

- Use diagrams to understand and de-mystify sections of Perambulations
- Use your Smartphone, Tablet or E-Reader so you always have your Work available.
- Look for rhythmic language to help you develop your knowledge of the Work

Chapter 6
Chapter of Improvement

Introduction

If you're really serious about Ritual, even if you only want to do one Ceremony to establish yourself in the Chapter, it is impossible to understate the importance of Chapter of Improvement.

CoI comes in many forms. Many Chapters have a dedicated CoI that meets regularly. Some of these are well organised, well planned and well-structured affairs that take the Ritual very seriously and endeavour to produce excellent renditions of the Ceremonies.

Some are less systematic in their approach, perhaps equally concerned with beer drinking as delivering faultless Ritual. Ironically, some of these CoI's actually deliver a pretty good result, because they do, by virtue of their inherently sociable environment, tend to attract regular attendance!

However, because Craft Lodges of Instruction often take priority over the Chapter, CoI is often an after-thought that gets inserted in the schedule only occasionally, when the Lodge of Instruction work is 'slow'.

Hopefully you will have access to one of these variants. Whatever the case, the Chapter of Improvement is a critical element for a Companion who is working his way through the various Offices. You can be certain that a Mason who does not regularly attend Chapter of Improvement will definitely struggle when (and if) he reaches the Principal's Chairs, which is a shame because your First Principal's Year is the pinnacle of your Chapter Masonry career. It should be an enjoyable experience for you, but more particularly it should be a pleasure for the other Companions. A poorly rehearsed MEZ (they do happen) can sometimes be an uncomfortable embarrassment, especially if your Chapter regularly welcomes Visitors.

So even if Ritual is not your main mission in life (and it needn't be), if you are serious about becoming Z of your Chapter you should really make an effort to attend Chapter of Improvement regularly, starting as early as you can.

Chapter of Improvement can be a lot of fun, once you get used to it. Masons are usually a welcoming bunch, though of course the Chapter also has its fair share of politicians and peacocks! There are many Chapters where attendance at Chapter of Improvement is mandatory if you want to be considered for progress through the Offices. This is fine if your Chapter is well-subscribed and there is competition for offices. In this case, you really have no option but to fall in line and attend regularly, otherwise you will either be systematically overlooked, or just forgotten about. Out of sight, out of mind, as the saying goes.

How to Get Offered the Work You Want

There's plenty of variation in the ways that Chapters 'allocate' the work to their Officers and Companions.

Some Chapters have a 'Standing Committee' or 'General Purposes Committee' which meets a few weeks before each Regular Chapter Meeting in order to plan the proceedings. Others rely on the regular PZ's meetings which are often hurried affairs just before the Chapter Meeting opens. If you intend to make your way as an active Ritualist in your Chapter, it is well worthwhile to attend the Committee meetings if you're allowed within your Chapter By-Laws. The allocation of the work may be decided autonomously by the Principals, maybe under advisement from the Secretary (Scribe E), and where there is a strong and active Chapter of Improvement, the Preceptor will undoubtedly contribute his advice as to who amongst the Companions is potentially equipped to participate in different parts of the Ceremony.

The problem seems to be that often these committees only meet a month or so ahead of the meeting, and that really doesn't allow enough time for a you to learn a piece of Ritual from a standing start. This is perhaps one reason why the same old faces pop up in many Chapters, especially when it comes to the various Lectures, Certificate presentations and so on, because a month may only be enough time for someone to revise a large Ceremony they have learned before.

So, you have to find a way to get more warning. My recommendation is that you approach the Preceptor of your Chapter of Improvement, and seek out his advice. You might perhaps tell him that you've been thinking about a Ceremony that you would like to try at a FUTURE Chapter meeting, and ask him to advise you on whether it should be Ceremony A or Ceremony B?

In the case where the Chapter does not have a formal committee, it's in your best interests to push yourself forwards in whatever way you can, in order to be considered for the Work. In small Chapters, just ask everyone who looks like they have some authority.

But it's OK to be less ambitious in the beginning. Think about the Work that your Chapter will perform over the coming, say, six to twelve months. What is the succession of Candidates coming through?

Can you see, for example, an Exaltation Ceremony about four to six months away? If you have been working on the example Historical Lecture, approach the Third Principal well in advance and ask if he would be willing to allow to you to take a shot at it! It has no perambulations or demonstrations involved (just some pointing). It would be a good choice for the novice Ritualist.

You Can't Make It To Chapter of Improvement?

If you find that you have joined a Chapter whose Chapter of Improvement schedule conflicts with your other responsibilities, it may be practical for you to find another Chapter of Improvement nearby which fits better with your work or family life. This is not at all unusual. You will be welcomed as a Companion, and if you clearly communicate the situation to the Preceptor of your own Chapter of Improvement, it will usually work out OK.

Although you will not be able to participate directly, both the Domatic and Aldersgate Chapters of Improvement, the bodies nominated as responsible for the maintenance and demonstration of the Royal Arch Ritual, continue to meet weekly at Freemasons Hall in Great Queen Street, London. The usual form is that they demonstrate the Exaltation every week, and the Installation once a month.

Details about their calendars and how to book may be found online.

The ideal Chapter of Improvement is more like a little club, perhaps meeting in a side room at the Masonic Centre, or in the back room of a pub (where some say Masonry originated!). I'm going to assume that your Chapter has a CoI, or shares one with other Chapters in the locality, so you already know how things work. Instead, it makes more sense to focus on how to get the best out of Chapter of Improvement, because it is by far the best (and maybe the only) opportunity to boost your Ritual performance in the company of your peers.

Chapter of Improvement Benefits

Chapter of Improvement is not for Learning Ritual prose; hopefully you have understood that if you have followed the instructions thus far: you need to do this on your own or privately with help from other Companions. You go to Chapter of Improvement to practice.

The conventional functions which a Chapter of Improvement delivers are these.

- Perambulations; Chapter of Improvement provides the only realistic environment for you to practice the 'walking about' parts of the Ceremony. In fact, the first time you attempt a Ceremony (probably as an Assistant Sojourner) which requires perambulations, the Ritual Book will probably not be much help to you. Although the Book does give reasonably precise instructions on the perambulations, unless you are very familiar with the layout of the Temple, it's unlikely that you will be able to memorize these important movements from text alone.

- Passwords and Salutes; These are not written out in the Ritual book, but are passed down by verbal or demonstration means, so the only places you will see and hear them are in the Chapter itself, or in the Chapter of Improvement. You can ask a more experienced Companion to give you the passwords you might need to learn for a specific Ceremony, but of course you are bound by your Obligations to keep them secret and not write them down, so Chapter of Improvement is really the only place to become familiar with these important words and actions.

- Sequence; how the whole Ceremony fits together, and then fits into the context of the overall meeting. By attending Chapter of Improvement you will get to observe the mechanics of how the Chapter works through the Summons, as well as the Opening and Closing Ceremonies. Familiarity with the sequences will be a great help to your confidence in the Chapter itself.

- Questions; At Chapter of Improvement, whilst there are protocols to be observed (it should be run like a proper Chapter Meeting) it is always possible to approach any other Companion with questions you might struggle to ask in the formal setting of the Chapter itself. Even the most senior Freemason will have time for you at Chapter of Improvement, and you can learn a lot of valuable stuff.

Some Chapters of Improvement hold what are called

'Officers Nights' in the last few weeks before the Meeting proper. The idea of an Officers Night is that all the Officers, and anyone else who is taking part in the Ceremonies at the forthcoming meeting, can come to the Chapter of Improvement and have a complete rehearsal of the whole Meeting. Sometimes it is the only opportunity to work with the other Officers, because not everyone can get to Chapter of Improvement regularly.

If you are participating in a Ceremony, you must make every effort to attend at least one Officers Night at your Chapter of Improvement so that you are comfortable with your part and role, and everyone trusts you.

Floorwork Homework

If you have a Sojourner's job to do and you need to practice the Ceremony including the perambulations but you cannot make it to Chapter of Improvement regularly, find a way to rehearse at home or in a room somewhere private.

By now you should understand the layout of the Chapter, with the Principals in the E, the Scribe N in the S, the Sojourners in the W, and the Scribe E's Table in the North. Nominate some bits of furniture to be those positions, and walk and talk the Ceremony around the room. Once you have gone through it a couple of times, you should easily be able to remember where you need to go at each stage, whilst you can practice the words and the salutes as well. You can easily do this on your own, and it will allow you to hit the ground running each time you go to Chapter of Improvement.

By all means, use the drawings or diagrams we explored earlier to help you remember the floor work.

PS Learning the Exaltation Ceremony

For a PS doing it for the first time, the Exaltation Ceremony lends itself best to be learned out of sequence. Before we explore that, we should take another look at the whole Ceremony, and deconstruct it into its four main sections so that you can understand the schedule;

1. Entrusting the Candidate; for this you will leave the Temple, and since it's the Candidate's first encounter with Royal Arch Masonry, you need to be slick and rehearsed. The only other person who can help you with prompts is the Janitor.

2. The Exaltation Ceremony; in your role as PS, you will be in control of the Candidate throughout this part, similarly to a Working Deacon in Craft. There are a few words to learn, specifically for the raising of the Candidate, but everything else in this part of the Ceremony involves your perambulations and instructing the Candidate to perform the actions required of him. You should apply all the techniques previously explained, in particular you really need to watch this Ceremony at least once or twice before you try it for yourself, and Chapter of Improvement is pre-requisite for you to rehearse it. The explanation of this section was given previously in Chapter 3, with the methodology for remembering and practising the floor work.

3. Three MMs from Babylon; this section is a dialogue with the MEZ, who will ask you questions which you

must answer according to the Ritual Book. You have one monologue of around 260 words ("We would scorn to be descended...") which is central to this section. There are no significant perambulations.

4. The Return of the Sojourners; this is the climax of the Ceremony and the biggest of your 'performances'. It begins with a 600 word Lecture and transitions to a series of perambulations which you will perform with other Chapter Officers.

So, the system for you to learn the PS Work at Exaltation, using all the strategies and techniques explained in this book, is as follows;

- Learn the big monologues first. These form around 75% of the Ceremony, but once you have them, you have your 'anchors' and it's much easier to learn the other parts.
    - o Entrusting the Candidate
    - o Three MM's from Babylon (which are actually answers to Z's questions)
    - o Return of the Sojourners (the big one).
- Next, learn the perambulations in Section 2, the Exaltation itself.
    - o You will need some rehearsal time at CoI; however you can use the diagram in Chapter 3 to practise at home.
- Now you have 90% of the work under your belt. The remaining parts will need Chapter of Improvement;
    - o Sharing the Name
    - o Re-Clothing

- Assisting with the Investiture

Performance Practice

When you are learning and preparing of the Monologues, or Lectures, for example, you will do most of the learning work alone, and in your head. If you have followed the recommendations and systems in the earlier Chapters, you should have mastered memorizing your work, and should now be quite comfortable speaking the Work out loud (as long as nobody's around to listen)!

But in order to start to prepare for the performance itself, it's important that you find opportunities to practice your 'recital' in something approaching the context of a real Chapter Meeting, and that is where Chapter of Improvement is particularly useful.

You will be encouraged to perform your work as an integral part of the Ceremony being rehearsed in Chapter of Improvement, so you will not only get to try out the performance aspect, but also you will get used to the way your part fits into the whole. Details like where you will be sitting before the DC collects you, where you will stand for your performance, and what happens afterwards, will all improve your confidence on the day and help you to ensure that your participate is smooth and seamless.

Posture and Delivery

People will only notice if you are awkward or unconventional. If you seem comfortable, they will feel comfortable too.

So in the early days of your career as a Ritualist, it makes more sense to worry less about the fine details of posture and delivery, and make the process as simple as possible.

- Stand up straight, but natural, and try to relax your body.
- Speak clearly, at a moderate speed. Keep breathing, pause often.
- If it helps, wave your hands around!

These three elements can be your basic 'rules'. If you can stick to them, you will accomplish the mission. Later on, you can add nuance and gesture, if you feel so inclined, but for now all that matters is that people notice you because of the accuracy and fluency of the Ritual you deliver.

So, work on finding a natural relaxed stance at Chapter of Improvement, and at home when you rehearse. Tension in the shoulders is a manifestation of stress; likewise if you forcefully relax your shoulders, the stress will dissipate, so practice like this;

- Stand up straight, whatever that means to you.
- Close your eyes for a moment
- Focus your attention on the muscles in your shoulders and neck
- Inhale deeply, then exhale slowly, whilst. you
- Push out the tension and let your shoulders drop (don't hunch forwards)
- Open your eyes and notice how relaxed you have become in just a few seconds.

Once you have tried it a few times, start practicing without closing your eyes. Before long you will find that you can relax really easily and virtually on-demand.

For your information, this is part of the basic method

behind self-hypnosis.

Pronunciation and Projection

The simple instruction here is that people need to be able to hear you and understand what you are communicating. So there are two things you need to practice;

- Pronouncing the words correctly
- Speaking Clearly

Maybe you already speak like a BBC newsreader, or perhaps you have a broad regional accent (which may be from somewhere else in the country.) Perhaps you have a foreign accent, or a speech impediment. Whatever the case, you owe it to your audience to do your best to deliver well-spoken Ritual. You shouldn't be thinking about changing the way you speak, or trying to be someone you're not, but this is 'Presentation-Speak' and everyone can do it. It's that slightly 'posher' version of your own voice that you might use if, say, the Queen came round for tea one day! It's your 'Telephone Voice'. It's your 'Interview Voice'

As far as clear speech is concerned, you need to work this out based on the best you can be whilst still feeling relatively relaxed whilst speaking. The biggest challenge to clear speech, or more particularly the fluency of it, is poor recall. If you are struggling to remember what to say next, you have not put enough attention into the early memorization task. This programme is tailored towards a fixed chronological timetable, which requires you to complete the three stages sequentially and completely. When you do this, you are able to recite the Ceremony naturally and fluently, which is the core of a confident performance.

Here is a good definition of Confidence; 'Competence Delivered'.

Performance Pressure

You may also discover the first couple of times that you perform your Work before a Chapter of Improvement audience, that although you thought you were word-perfect in the shower that morning, it's a different story altogether when you do it for real.

This may be your first taste of 'Performance Pressure', sometimes termed 'Choking' and it can be very frustrating. Knowing something doesn't necessarily mean a person will remember it properly when faced with the presence of an audience and the need to do a good job.

So the first step in overcoming the tendency to choke is to simulate the performance situation and re-run the exercise as many times as possible, and the only place where this is really viable is in the Chapter of Improvement.

You may be shy or nervous; however it's really important to push (respectfully) to get your opportunities. The more rehearsals you can achieve in the weeks preceding the actual meeting, the better prepared you will be the first time you stand up to work in Open Chapter.

Don't be shy. Just find your allies, be ready, and take it on.

Your Chapter of Improvement is a Masonic Chapter in all but the most formal sense. It is specifically designed to provide instruction and practise in the Ritual. You should use it as such, because the first time you are able to deliver your Ritual to an acceptable standard at Chapter of Improvement, you will know that you are ready to do exactly the same thing in the Temple. Your Chapter of Improvement audience is likely to be a lot more critical than the Chapter Meeting itself, so if you can do it there, you can do it anywhere!

Summary

- Try to immerse yourself in Chapter of Improvement; it will pay big dividends.
- Attend Standing Committee to get the 'inside track' on forthcoming Work.
- If your own Chapter of Improvement is inconvenient, join one nearby that works for you.
- Rehearse the perambulations at home, and then practice them at Chapter of Improvement with the team.
- Be ambitious, especially if you are getting closer to the Principals Chairs.
- Use Chapter of Improvement to understand the pattern and sequence of the whole Ceremony.
- Don't get hung up on Posture; find a comfortable relaxed style that works for you.
- Teach yourself to Relax on-demand.
- Develop your 'Telephone Voice' to speak clearly and enunciate.
- Remember; "Confidence is Competence Delivered"

Chapter 7
Rehearsal

Quick Check

Let's briefly re-cap where you are; So far, we've been following a sequence which should have gone like this;

Observation: You visited a Chapter, or one of the major Chapters of Improvement to see 'your' Work being performed in a real situation, to get a feel for the context, and to "Measure the Work".

Cramming (Memorizing): You used all the techniques and short-cuts, finding out which ones worked for you, and you 'crammed' the Work into your memory. You established your daily practice routines.

Polishing: You then employed another set of techniques and strategies to iron out all the kinks and to get as close as possible to a perfect rendition of your Work.

Chapter of Improvement: Hopefully you'll have had the chance to try out your Work in Chapter of Improvement, and you'll have a good feel for how close you are to being able to deliver it for real.

By now, you should be around three-quarters of the way through the allocated timetable for the particular Work you are due to deliver at your next Chapter Meeting. The final phase of this learning exercise is to concentrate on the performance aspects.

Repetition

I hope that you are still following the systems you learned in the first Stage, to continue to mentally and verbally recite your Work at every opportunity. The more of this simple practice you do, the less you risk forgetting a word or drying up when it comes to the big day.

As you practice, you will notice the improvements yourself. At first, having broken the passage into sections, you had to think about how to move from the end of one section to the start of the next, and what order the sentences came in. By now, you should have virtually eliminated that conscious effort, and you should be moving seamlessly from one section to the next, so that the parts have become a whole.

Even now, it's important to continue to check yourself against the Book, perhaps using one of the techniques we explored in Stage Two, to ensure that you haven't picked up any bad habits. When you're rehearsing in Chapter of Improvement, unless you are very specific or the Preceptor is an absolute stickler, you may pass over small mistakes such as single words or re-arranged phrases, without anyone pulling you up on it. So it's important to keep checking the veracity of your own memory. You have all the tools, so use them.

If you are learning a Lecture, you may only need to take a look at the Book every few days, or if a small question about accuracy arises in your own mind (this happens).

If you are learning Work which involves perambulations, particularly as PS, then the way to use the book is to cover the page with something like a business card, which you can slide down as you work your way through the Ceremony. This allows you to read and understand the flow of the Ceremony itself, identifying the cues for you to do or say something, then rehearse your part before you uncover that particular part of the page.

This repetitious recital, whether it's silent or spoken, simply drives the prose deeper into your subconscious, where it will remain, in some form, more or less forever. This is what you are trying to achieve, because although the primary intention of this book is to get you through your first Chapter Ritual performance, the most important by-product is that once you learn a Ceremony for the first time, if you do it right, it will be there for you to revise and deliver again in the future, with much less work.

It's also important, as we previously discussed, that you perform the WHOLE piece as often as possible, in order to balance your familiarity with the later portion against the earlier portion, which you learned first.

Serious Rehearsal

This is the part of the process where most mistakes are made, so we'll put some strategies in place to ensure that doesn't happen to you.

Let's make the assumption that you still have a few weeks to go before the Big Day, and that you've tried at least one full run through of your Work in the Chapter of Improvement. If that went well, just keep doing what you're doing and you'll be fine.

Some people will have discovered a lot about themselves at Chapter of Improvement, and you may be apprehensive about how you are going to get yourself ready to do it for real. Here is where the Ritualists separate themselves from the crowd, because they know that the Performance aspect is where the real Work is done.

You need to Seriously Rehearse, and you need to do it at least once (probably twice) every single day in the lead up to the Meeting.

The simplest recommendation here is that you need to shut yourself away, with no distractions, and deliver your Work, out loud, and completely. Find somewhere private, which may be as simple as closing your office door at lunchtime, or taking a walk around the block. If you are a traveler, hotel rooms are perfect because they are usually soundproof, you are usually alone, and you will usually have time to spare.

The critical point is that you are not just reciting, you are Rehearsing. You need to stand up, exactly as you will be in the Chapter, and you need to speak at full volume, exactly as you will need to do on the day. You may find that once you start to put a little effort into the diction and delivery, you'll suddenly discover a few small places where your memorisation may be weak. This is a great opportunity to address those, and you will be able to fix them really quickly.

The key benefit of this rehearsal style, apart from practising the monologue, is that you will start to use your aural sense (of the ear) which will open a new channel into your memory. You will start to train yourself how the Ritual sounds to you when you are performing it, and this will enable you to more truly appreciate the rhythms and patterns in the language, which might have eluded you in the earlier phases.

When you rehearse the Ritual out-loud, you are doubling or even trebling the effectiveness over a silent recital. So do it as often as you can, and be as authentic as possible.

A couple of points;

Firstly, I have heard of people recommend using a mirror to aid rehearsal. Frankly, it may work for some people, but I can't really see the point.

In the Rehearsal phase, you are trying to internalise the processes of memory recall, to focus your senses on the main skills needed to retain and repeat a complex sequence of language. Watching yourself do this is, to me, an unnatural situation and a potential distraction from the focus you are trying to achieve. There won't be a mirror in the Chapter, and the objective here is to try to replicate as closely as possible the real situation that you will be in.

Secondly, although I eschew the use of audio recording as a primary learning tool, in the Rehearsal Stage it can be very useful as a method of self-critique.

You don't need a separate recorder (our Ancient Companions called it a Dictaphone). Most smart-phones are equipped with a high quality voice recorder, so use it if you think it will help.

Do it like this;
- Rehearse the passage once or twice, out loud, to the best of your ability. Get into the mind-set that you are preparing to record it, so that you are working up to a peak.
- Set up your phone (or other recording device) so that you don't have to hold it. Use your hands-free

- earphones instead of the phone's own microphone, if you can.
- When you feel ready, start the Voice Recorder and deliver the Work. In the beginning it's OK to break it into sections if it's a big piece like the Exaltation. But try to get through each section without pausing. If you make an error, don't dwell on it; just keep moving (because that's the way you want to deal with any mistakes when you do it for real).
- Finally, play back the recording, and have your Book open whilst you listen, so that you can check yourself for any grammatical errors that might have registered whilst you were reciting it.
- Now delete that recording. Repeat the process as many times as you need to. You will probably get bored with the repetition, but that's a good sign because that will indicate that you are ready to move on.

Rehearsing With a Partner

On any given evening, lights burn brightly from the windows of garden sheds all over this land…

It's useful to have these systems and techniques for learning and rehearsing on your own, however rehearsing with a partner can be really helpful in this stage too. I know many Companions who visit each other's homes in order to rehearse Ritual in front of a friendly audience of one. This is a great idea and I can't recommend it enough. It's not practical for everyone, but you'd be surprised how many people will gladly invite you round to rehearse, if you make it known that that is what you are looking for. And of course there's always a cup of tea or the odd bottle of beer, though I would caution you against attempting to rehearse anything serious whilst sampling another Companion's home-made wine!

If you are fortunate enough to have a friend in the Chapter who you can rehearse with, make sure you agree to be brutally honest about each other's performances, because you need honest and timely critique throughout the process.

In The Car

If you get to spend a lot of time on your own in the car, you have a great opportunity to become really good at Masonic Ritual. You can practice to your heart's content, so don't waste the opportunity.

Boring motorway journeys are the best. As with the earlier learning strategies, it's a good idea to pre-plan your in-car rehearsal time. This stops you procrastinating. Maybe you know that a particular radio programme starts or ends at a certain time, so build your schedule around that. You really need to turn off your phone, and turn off the radio too, because even at low volume it will disturb your attention.

Of course you can't read or check the Book whilst you are driving, so it lends itself to doing larger run-throughs when you've already learned most of the Ceremony. However, because you can't check the Book, it forces you to use memory recall whenever you hit a snag, which will help to sharpen your powers.

Running through the same piece two or three times, although it can be a bit boring, is a really good way to make progress whilst you are driving, and you might be surprised about how much more you remember by the third time than the first time. Remember, Masonic Language is about flow, rhythm and sequence, and these attributes really start to deliver when you are rehearsing out loud.

Earlier, we discussed how rehearsing 'out-loud' has a multiplying effect on your progress. It also has hugely beneficial effects to your confidence.

Your Targets

There are many factors which go into a great performance, probably enough to fill another book. For the purpose of this, however, here are the three most significant attributes which you should be targeting for your Ritual delivery;

- Competence
- Confidence
- Sincerity

Competence

If you have followed the systems and processes in the book thus far, you will have achieved a level of competence which should enable you to be able to achieve a basic recital of the Work without serious errors. You may not be totally perfect, but that shouldn't concern you at this stage. If you can get the words out, more or less in the right order, then your competence is established. Masonry being a progressive science, it is only logical that competence should be one of the key underlying attributes of the next (and probably most important) factor.

Confidence

Remember, Confidence is defined as 'Competence Delivered'.

First and foremost, don't confuse nerves with lack of confidence! There are many Companions who have decades of Ritual experience under their belts, who still get nervous. However they don't lack confidence because they know that they have the competence to deliver the Ceremony, having done it before.

So it's okay to feel a little bit nervous. I mentioned earlier in the book the commonality between excitement and anxiety. Both of these are physical reactions of the body to the anticipation of what lies ahead. They are not quite the same, but are sufficiently similar as to be virtually interchangeable based on context. In other words, the body and mind react more or less the same way to the anticipation of a pleasant forthcoming event as an unpleasant one, but a person's perception of whether the event is going to be pleasant and positive versus unpleasant and negative has a determining effect on that person's perception of why and how they feel what they feel.

So, how is this relevant to confidence?

In a number of talking therapies such as cognitive behavioural therapy (CBT) and some branches of hypnotherapy, a technique known as re-framing is often used to teach the subject how to take control of these physical feelings and alter the underlying context, so that a feeling of anxiety or apprehension may actually be re-framed into one of positive anticipation or even excitement. Of course we don't have time here or the techniques to hand to start messing around in psychology, however just the simple fact that you now have this knowledge may enable you, if you are of a nervous disposition, to help yourself.

One of the common factors of both anxiety and excitement is that they both act on other systems in the body in order to focus energy and concentration where it is needed. Everyone knows about "fight or flight" which is our ancient genetic response to fear or danger, where a huge blast of stimulating chemicals, particularly adrenaline, surges into the bloodstream in order to enable the body to channel all of its resources and energy towards the faculties that are most important in that threatening situation. Vision, response, hearing and other vital capabilities can become temporarily enhanced, whilst digestion and other non--essential services will be momentarily suspended.

So a nervous disposition can also work to your advantage. Of course nobody expects you to be frightened for your life when you're going into the Chapter to perform some Ritual! However, if you are able to do so, you can perhaps utilise any nervous anticipation you may be feeling to focus yourself on the really important aspects of the task ahead.

So, let's analyse if you are areas in which confidence is important.

Will I Remember the Words?

Almost every Ritualist hits a roadblock during a performance at one time or another. Don't be frightened of this; it's no reflection on your ability or your efforts. It just happens from time to time, even to the best of us. That is why you need to have a good understanding with your prompter. Trying to perform Ritual in the Temple without a prompter is like the flying trapeze without a safety net. You may never need it, but if you get a snag halfway through and there's nothing there to fall back on, or nobody to catch you, it will be messy! The next chapter explains how you should work with your prompter to ensure that your safety net is in place without being intrusive.

What Happens If I Mess Up Perambulations Or Salutes?

Usually nothing! If you make a big mistake which is liable to disrupt the Ceremony, you can be sure that someone nearby will pull you up discreetly. Just make sure that you are listening to what's going on around you if you are doing PS Work, because almost every other Companion in the Chapter has been in Office at one time or another, and some of them will actually remember how to do it right!

Of course it is the Director of Ceremonies' responsibility to ensure that movement around the Chapter is conducted correctly. If you are in the PS Office it's always a good idea to have a good relationship with the DC. You should let him know before each Ceremony if you have any particular concerns, or are confused about where you should be or what you should be doing. Remember, as we said earlier, Freemasons love to help each other so never be afraid to ask! Because no matter how well drilled you were at Chapter of Improvement, once you step onto the Temple floor, it's a different dynamic.

In terms of how these elements affect your confidence, they should not. As we have discussed many times in this book, it's very rare to see a perfect Ceremony (and it can sometimes be pretty boring if you get one). So you should not allow these small issues to affect the central plank of your confidence going into the Work.

Confidence-Building Techniques

If you subscribe to the earlier definition of Confidence as 'Competence Delivered', then you will have understood the importance of building a good performance on solid foundations, by applying time and effort to thoroughly learning the Work. You can eliminate almost all the normal obstacles to faultless execution by simply Knowing Your Stuff.

Another aspect of confidence is the entirely natural concern about how people perceive us.

There are a couple of things you should know: many people who appear to be confident in public are actually quite shy underneath. The outward confidence they display is a subconscious strategy that they have developed in order to deal with their shyness. The strategy is often based around commitment to a process: in other words they use a rigid framework of commitment for tasks, and by focusing on the task and shutting out distractions they are able to do it well. Consequently they successfully de-link the task from their core personality. You may sometimes see this with actors, who appear to be fantastically confident on-stage or on-screen but when you see them on a TV chat show they are shy, or even gauche.

Many, many people have some element of shyness or insecurity hard-wired into their personalities. However you can utilise this knowledge to your advantage when it comes to performing Ritual. When you step out onto the squared pavement you may also be stepping out of your own comfort zone, so it's important that you have made a commitment to do that. It's a little bit like suspending reality for a short time. You leave any imperfections, shyness, and lack of confidence, insecurities, or any other negative traits that you may possess, outside the door of the Chapter. There is no great trick to this, you just need to take yourself to one side, take a couple of deep breaths, and let it out.

The 'Line of Commitment'

Sports psychologists use a technique called "Line of Commitment" when they are working with individual sportsmen and women.

Many sportsmen and women use visualisation techniques, including the 'Line of Commitment'. It's your own personal 'start line' that puts you firmly in control of the task ahead. You mentally create and physically cross that line only when you are comfortable that you have martialled all your internal resources to accomplish the task.

Golfers are great exponents of this technique; just watch Tiger or any of the top guys, how they act when they step onto the tee. Everyone knows that the great golfers claim to visualise the shot they want before they hit it for real.

You can often see them also looking at their imaginary Line of Commitment, before they take a breath, step up, and split the fairway. So that seems to work.

Adapting this technique for our purposes, you should follow a sequence as follows;

- Find somewhere private that you can relax and rehearse.
- To begin, confirm your Competence. Remind yourself that you have LEARNED the Ritual to the

best of your ability. Of course, we would all like longer to practice, but you got what you were given, and you used it wisely.
- Are you familiar with the 'performance environment' (the Temple), based on your visits and observations of the Ceremony being performed?
- For Work with Perambulations; have you done the complete Ceremony at Chapter of Improvement?
- For Lectures, have you successfully done a complete delivery to an audience, even if it is only one person?

If you have stuck to your initial plan and the process in this book, you should be able to answer Yes to these questions. You 'Know Your Stuff'. This is a given fact.

- The next part of the exercise requires you imagine yourself in the performance environment. You may be able to close your eyes and visualise, or you may be more kinaesthetic and be able to 'feel' how it will be. Whatever your own modality, try to use it to 'get into the zone'.
- See what you see, hear what you hear, feel how you feel, and try to identify any part of you that has concerns or questions.
- In your imagination, draw a white line on the floor in front of your feet, about a meter wide and ten centimetres thick. That is your Line of Commitment.
- The next step you take will be over that Line, and once you have crossed it, you will have committed to start your performance.

Try it: when you have everything ready to go, Step over the Line and go straight into your Ritual.

Use this technique regularly in rehearsal, and then take it with you to the Chapter on the day of the Meeting. Never cross your Line of Commitment until you are totally ready.

Control of the Environment

One of the key attributes of the Performance Environment is that it is controllable, by you. Although there are other people in the Temple, they are all 'trained' to conform to the protocols, which means that, barring any major aberration by another Officer in the Ceremony, nothing unexpected is likely to occur. There will be no surprises.

Allied to this, the majority of your audience is assimilating the Ceremony as a complete event, and is unlikely to be monitoring your personal performance in anything other than a general way. The remaining minority is those who are also involved in the Ceremony with you and they are pre-occupied by whatever their next contribution is going to be, so they are not overly concerned with your performance.

If this is going to be your first real attempt at Ritual, you already have a lot of support inherent in your audience. Everyone will want you to do well, but everyone will also make certain allowances for you first time out, so accept that benevolence and cut yourself some slack. As was explained earlier, fluency and sincerity are the most noticeable attributes of a Ritual performance, so don't get hung up linguistic accuracy.

You control your environment, you know your stuff, and

the audience is on your side. It's all good!

Sincerity

Have you ever heard it said of someone "He could make the telephone directory sound interesting"?

Sincerity is the quality that will ensure you are never remembered as being boring, which was a rule on the first page of this book. Sincerity is defined as "freedom from deceit, hypocrisy, or duplicity; probity in intention or in communicating; earnestness". It basically says that you mean what you say.

Like a suntan, sincerity can cover a multitude of sins! It's another Secret Weapon for the Ritualist, because sincerity tends to negate criticism, spoken or unspoken, in your audience. If you come across as sincere, people will be distracted from the technical precision of what you are doing, and will get a nice warm feeling about you and your performance. Not only will the reception of your performance be enhanced, but you stand a much better chance of getting away with any imperfections or ad-libs.

The easiest way to sound and feel sincere when you are delivering Ritual is to use intonation in your voice. Test yourself by extracting a few key sentences from the Ritual, sentences that carry some specific meaning, and rehearse them separately, trying different patterns of intonation to place stress on some words or phrases. Inject slightly longer pauses in some places. Play around with the language until it begins to feel natural to you. Remember, you're still in learning mode, and the sound of your own voice will register and resonate inside, and add layers of texture and colour on top of the basic language you have memorised.

I don't propose that you 'manufacture' sincerity when you're in the rehearsal stage of the Ritual process, but more that you relax yourself into it. You deserve the opportunity to add a little emotion into your performance, because you have worked very hard to get to this point. If you can introduce genuine sincerity, you will enjoy it more, and so will your audience.

Progress Check

The key idea behind this book was to provide the novice, aspiring, frustrated, or failed Ritualist with a structured method of learning and delivering an acceptable Ritual performance in the Chapter. The main purpose of encouraging you to take part in the Ritual is to enhance your enjoyment of Masonry and fulfil your potential as a Freemason.

You have completed the Competence part in the early Stages. You know your stuff, so there's nothing for you to be concerned about in that department. With respect to your Confidence, if you can buy into the principle of 'Competence Delivered', you have a sound basis on which to proceed.

However, for some people, confidence is a bigger issue in their lives, one that can hold them back in terms of career, relationships, fitness and health, and lots of other areas. Freemasonry is an excellent forum in which to build confidence and carry it into your normal life.

Sincerity is something for you to experiment with, finding the style that best fits with your feeling for the Ritual and your desire to express yourself during the performance. It is well worth investing a little time in this area, because it can have a massive effect on how you are perceived as a Ritualist.

Of course, all of these are progressive attributes which will grow and develop as you do more and more Ritual in your Chapter.

Summary

- Keep your Daily Routines going. The more you practice, the more competent you'll be.
- Aim for at least one complete rehearsal each day.
- Speak out loud whenever you can. It has a multiplying effect on your fluency.
- Rehearse with a partner whenever possible, but be brutal with each other!
- If you're a PS, enlist the help and guidance of the DC.
- Once again, remember; "Confidence is Competence Delivered"

Chapter 8
The Day of the Meeting

Performance Day

Hopefully you have followed the system in this book, and if you have you should be 'ready to go' well in advance of the day of the Meeting.

Even assuming that you're fully rehearsed, it's human nature to doubt yourself, even if this is irrational, so you will definitely still be looking to improve your confidence towards a solid performance on the day itself.

You are Ready, though you might not believe it!

Weekday or Saturday?

If you are lucky enough to be a member of a Saturday Chapter, you may have a slight advantage, since you probably don't have to go to work on the day of the Chapter Meeting. That will give you chance to do at least one proper run through, out loud, and perhaps have someone give you a final check-up. It's not too late to make a few small adjustments. Remember, the Ritual evolves in your brain, as you become more accustomed to it, so you will constantly add expression and intonation to your Work as each small section becomes permanently implanted in your long-term memory.

However if that is not an option, for example if you are

attending a Chapter meeting on a working day, just stick to the system we've been practising in the run up to the meeting.

If your Work is large, you will have figured out the particular passages that worry you, so practice those, and only those; in the bathroom, in the car, on the train, or wherever you do your private rehearsal. Remember the point of this in the latter phase is to reinforce your powers of recall. So don't worry if you are still stumbling over a few words, just keep going over your suspect passages, working them down one by one until you are relaxed, or as close as you are likely to be!

Whatever your situation, you need to find an opportunity for one complete run-through before you go into the Chapter. This is no longer about you improving your performance; it is all about you demonstrating to yourself exactly how competent you are, so that you can add that knowledge to your confidence. This final run-through can often be the most important step in finally fixing any niggling problems you have, because you know it's the last time you'll rehearse, so you tend to focus on what's really important. You won't get another chance to fix anything, if you don't know it by now, you'll be completely at the mercy of your recall and your Prompter once you 'step off with your left foot' as it were.

Set Yourself a Deadline

Today, you need to set a cut-off point for yourself. The deal you make with yourself is this; once you pass the cut-off point, you will not attempt to change anything about your performance. That's not to say that you can't carry on practising in your head, or even out loud if you can find the opportunity. But at your cut-off point, you have done all the learning you can do, and the version of the Work that you have at that moment is the version you are going to use.

If you are feeling very confident, you might decide that your cut-off point will be as soon as you leave the house to go to the meeting. At the other end of the scale you may choose your entrance into the Chapter as your cut-off point. It doesn't really matter, so long as you set your deadline and stick to it.

When you reach your cut-off point (maybe you can set another of those pesky vibrating alarms in your phone) you should momentarily stop whatever you are doing, take a breath, and do the relaxation exercise you learned earlier. In that moment, all the learning, the memorizing and the rehearsing is consigned to your archive, and all that should remain is the performance you are about to make.

The point of this technique is to ensure that you emphatically *close* the learning process. You should accept that, at that moment, you have done all you can and there is nothing else you can do, and then concentrate on getting yourself into the performance mind-set.

Travelling to the Chapter

Your journey to the Chapter may be your final chance for rehearsal. Maybe you are a member of a Provincial Chapter and you live nearby, in which case the short journey may be of little or no consequence. However, many Masons live some distance from their Chapters, and the journey is substantial.

We can't cover every possible permutation, so here are

some simple decisions that you might consider when travelling to a Chapter meeting where you are going to be delivering a substantial piece of Ritual.

Firstly the journey to the Chapter is perhaps the last and best opportunity to run through the Ceremony, so you may want to avoid hooking up with any of your other Companions, so you can travel into town alone. Alternately, you might want to be with someone who can test you on your final run through, in which case make sure it's someone who is smart enough to encourage you and support your confidence.

The second decision is usually whether to drive or take public transport. Of course, if you drive you can't drink, so that is a separate consideration. But in terms of your Ritual, driving allows you to recite out-loud, which of course is impossible on the bus or on the train.

For me, I will usually choose the driving option if I'm comfortable that I've mastered the work I'm doing and I just want to practice my delivery.

On the other hand, if I've hit some obstacles along the way, or if I've been asked to do something at short notice, then the journey to the Chapter is the last opportunity for me to work with the Book, in which case public transport or a taxi is the best option.

Complacency

You must avoid complacency: 'I did it before so it'll be fine this time.' Mental performance is a wildly variable state, depending on hormones, chemicals, sleep, general health and a whole raft of other contributory factors. It is not in the nature of the human condition to be completely consistent in anything, so don't risk it.

Alcohol

Here's a surprise; Masonry and Drinking are commonly practiced together (well, not at exactly the same time, but definitely on the same day). I'm sure there are Masonic Centres which don't have bars inside or pubs next door, but I haven't come across one yet!

Most of the Masons I know like a drink with their friends before and/or after the meeting, and I'm no different, so it would be disingenuous to insist that you avoid alcohol on a day where you are going to deliver Ritual in the Chapter.

However, I must tell you that I have, on occasions, seen defeat snatched from the jaws of victory by a Brother or Companion who had one too many before giving his performance. If you are naturally nervous, please avoid the temptation to use drinks before the meeting to relax, because it rarely works.

Often the problem is that Companions fail to eat properly before the meeting, maybe because they're saving themselves for the Festive Board. This is dangerous, because by the time you stand up in the Chapter to deliver your Ceremony, it may be seven or eight hours since breakfast time, and the effect of those couple of beers you had in the pub before the meeting will be greatly amplified. That's not to say that you will be obviously drunk in front of the Chapter (and you'll probably be forgiven for this) but it will almost definitely impair your intellectual powers, particularly your memory and your powers of recall.

I don't want to be a hypocrite, and I am certainly no advertisement for temperance myself, but as a general rule I would advise no more than one drink in advance of the meeting if you are going to be performing Ritual. There's plenty of time for 'relaxation' once your work is done!

The alternate to meeting at the pub on the day of your Ritual performance, and I have seen and done this numerous times, is to head over to the Temple and squeeze in some rehearsal time before everyone else gets there. Check with the Janitor that it's OK first.

Prompting

Many Chapters will have their own 'traditions' for Prompting. In some Chapters, there may be a complete ban on Ritual books in the Temple (three cheers!!!), in which case it will probably fall to the IPZ or another Senior Officer to be the Prompter from memory.

Irrespective, the most important advice is that you should speak to your nominated Prompter beforehand, and ensure that he has a clear understanding of how you will request prompts. Hopefully you can have this conversation at a Chapter of Improvement meeting, so that your Prompter has the opportunity to observe how you work, the speed of your delivery, the length of your pauses, and so on. The Ritualist and his Prompter are a team. A good Prompter will know exactly how to help you without interfering with your performance.

In my own Chapter, I have an understanding with the Scribe E, and the Companions know that he is my only Prompter when I am performing Ritual on the floor of the Chapter. He will never prompt me unless I indicate that I need help.

Why is this understanding important? Well, if you have trained your power of recall discussed earlier in this book you may sometimes need a slightly longer pause in order to find the next sentence, and you really don't want your Prompter to jump in whilst you are focused on digging deep inside for your words.

On Arrival

Don't expect that anyone is going to ask you about your Ritual once you arrive at the Chapter. Everyone is focused on their own Work for the day. If you need to have any conversations, for example with the DC, other working Officers, or even the MEZ, try to get there early and see them in plenty of time, because once the DC starts looking like he's about to form the Procession, your chance is gone and everyone will be too busy to speak to you.

Assuming that the Chapter Room or Temple is open and empty whilst the Companions are dressing for the meeting, it's always a good idea to go in and have a little rehearsal or run through, again just for re-assurance. In many Chapters, the DC will instruct working Officers to arrive early in order that a rehearsal of the floor work can be held, which is always a smart thing to do. That final run through is the last chance to pick up any little glitches, and for you it is also an ideal opportunity to re-confirm your competence.

If you are performing a Lecture from the floor, you should definitely try to 'walk the walk' to get from your seat to your performance position, so that you have a feel for how long it will take.

Next, you should practise the "Line of Commitment" technique you learned. Stand in position, breathe deeply, make a quick checklist of your competence and comfort, then take a short step forwards over your Line of Commitment and begin. It's unlikely that anyone will object if you start to rehearse out loud, even if it's only the first few words.

You should also practice your finish. Remember, in the Royal Arch there are no salutes during the meeting, as a court bow is the usual convention. When you are finished, for real, the DC or ADC will come and pick you up again and take you back to your seat. So once you have finished your work, you may need to stand still for a few seconds whilst the DC gets to you. Make sure you know which direction he will approach from, and which direction you should face while you wait. This is really just common sense, but its mastery of these little details that will boost your confidence and underpin your contribution to a seamless meeting.

Where to Sit

This is easy. If you are in Office, the decision is already made for you.

If you are not in office, and are being brought up to perform a Lecture, or another element of the Ceremony, you should talk to the DC before the meeting and ask him where he would like you to sit. He or his Assistant will be coming to pick you up in the course of their perambulations, so let the DC decide for you.

If he says he doesn't mind, it's a good idea to position yourself around half way between the DC's position and the point of Delivery, which will vary depending on the Ceremony .

Beginning and Ending a Lecture

Once you are placed in your position, you are in complete control of the starting point and the speed of delivery.

Remember what we practiced in Chapter 7: don't be tempted to speed up and rush your delivery.

Final Mental Rehearsal

Almost every Mason I ever met gets nervous before they deliver a Ceremony or a Ritual passage. This is particularly common for Lectures.

You would be unusual if you didn't have a few butterflies just before you get up; Remember the points about context; this is excitement. It's a good sign that you are comfortable that you are ready and fully rehearsed.

There's no hard and fast rule about continuing to practise silently during the meeting, because the situation varies enormously. However, since you have already confirmed your competence, it is most unlikely that you will gain any new benefits or make any amazing new discoveries at this late stage. Having passed your 'cut-off point', its fine to think about what you are going to do, but don't try to make any changes. Of course you will naturally think about the task ahead whilst you are waiting your turn, but you should trust yourself that you have the resources you need.

If you are silently rehearsing, and you find you have forgotten something, don't panic. This is common, because there is often some other distraction which is impacting on your focus. The learning process you have completed has solidified and consolidated your Work as a 'whole piece' in your memory. The out-loud rehearsing you did in Stage Three has also imprinted an audio-image, so when you get up to perform, your subconscious should be feeding you the words as a flow. You will remember even the things you are worried that you may have forgotten. You haven't forgotten anything!

If you are allowed to take your book into the Temple, it's fine to check it. But don't let anyone see you doing it!

Be Ready

Make sure you have read the summons, so that you know exactly where you are going to be in the running order. There's nothing worse than finding yourself semi-comatose in a Chapter Meeting when suddenly your name is called out and it's time for your Work, which you thought was happening later!

If you are being 'inserted' in a Ceremony, you should have practiced the sequence with the whole team at LoI. But if you're not sure, make sure you discreetly follow the Ceremony in your book, so that you're completely prepared when the time comes. You need to maintain your calm as much as possible.

Posture and Delivery

We agreed to keep this simple. You should have been able to work out your delivery 'style' in Chapter of Improvement, so there's no reason to change any of it at this stage. Three simple instructions;

- Stand up straight, be natural, and try to relax your body.
- Speak clearly, at a moderate speed. Keep breathing, pause often.
- Try not to wave your hands around too much!!

If you have stuck to the system in this book, you should have gone through the visualisation (or kinaesthetic simulation) of how it is going to be when you step up to begin, so you shouldn't have any shocks or surprises.

Good Luck!

Summary

- On Meeting Day, rehearse as many times as you can, starting with your Bathroom Routine.
- Plan your journey to give the right kind of rehearsal or practice time on the way.
- Avoid drinking before the Meeting: save it for later!
- Check in with your Prompter, so you're both on the same page.
- Try to get a 'walk through' in the Temple, before the meeting.
- Sit in the right place, stay relaxed, and be mentally and physically ready.
- When your turn comes, stand up straight and take a breath to relax
- Focus your resources and step over your Line of Commitment.

Chapter 9

Next Steps

The Day After

So, you did it! You taught yourself a Ceremony and you delivered it in the Chapter. I'm guessing that it went OK for you?

How Do You Feel?

Maybe you just feel relieved that it's over and done with, or maybe you really enjoyed the sense of achievement, because you really did do something special. Hopefully you didn't hate every minute of the process, and now you understand that a systematic approach can deliver a strong performance, you'll be ready for the next one.

Once the Festive Board is over, and you've been congratulated on a job well done, there's a new set of processes for you to follow, in order to take the best from the whole experience and apply it for the future.

First, when you go to bed on the night of the meeting, things may be different for you. For the last few weeks, every night has involved a systematic rehearsal of your Ritual, but tonight you're in the clear, right?

Wrong!

Being a participant in the Ritual of your Chapter involves

you building a library of Ceremonies in your memory, because it's a fair bet that you'll be called upon to do each one more than once. If your first encounter with the Work was as PS, for example, you'll probably have another chance to perform the same work again, either during the remainder of your year in the PS office, or as a stand-in at some future date, or even in another Chapter if you should expand your Masonry beyond your Mother Chapter sometime in the future.

So What Did You Learn?

In the immediate aftermath of a 'performance' it's a good idea to review what happened. I'd be very surprised if you are entirely happy with your performance. Maybe the things you expected to trip you up were actually fine, but you struggled with something unexpected? Maybe you thought (no, maybe you KNEW) that you'd followed the system and you'd thoroughly learned your words, but you still got stuck a couple of times and needed prompts?

Listen, don't worry about it. Unless it was a complete disaster, in which case let's go back a few steps and try it again, you have accomplished your first mission, and from here you can only get better.

Rule 1; Protecting Your Assets

You just spent several weeks learning a tricky passage or Ceremony, and the natural temptation is to say 'Phew' and forget about it for now.

However, now is the right time to weld this work into your memory, so that it will be there more easily the next time you need it. Masonry is a long game, and it's almost certain that you'll have several opportunities to revisit each part of the Ritual throughout your Chapter career.

By spending just a little more time on this Ritual now, you could save yourself many hours of re-learning in the future.

The pressure is off you. Hopefully nobody is expecting you to do this work again in the short term. If you enjoyed yourself this time, you'll probably want to take on something new and more challenging for your next outing. Whatever the case, it's a good time to protect what you just learned and delivered.

I recommend that for the next week or so, you find time to recite the work you just learned, at least once a day. Without the performance pressure, you'll be much more relaxed about it, and it will thoroughly cement itself into your long-term memory.

Simply put; until you get some new Work, keep practising the old Work.

Straight After the Meeting

The time to start is when you go to bed on the night of the meeting, when the performance itself is still fresh in your short-term memory. This gives you a golden opportunity to review it. Lie down in the dark, close your eyes, and replay the actual performance in your mind. You may be surprised to find that any mistakes or prompts will magically reappear, and you'll have a chance to analyse each one and add those analyses to the bank of information you already stored about this Ceremony whilst you were learning it.

I know it's the last thing you feel like doing right now, but I promise you that it will pay massive dividends down the line.

Acknowledge Your Strengths and Weaknesses

If you followed the method in this book so far, you'll know that the central core of this Ritual method is systematic organisation. In keeping with that, here are some key metrics you can check against your performance. If you're serious about improving for the next time (maybe you don't need to!) then you can score yourself against each criterion;

- Did you actually forget any of the passage(s)?
- Did you need prompts to get from one section to the next?
- Did you feel confident in the delivery?
- Do you think you were you boring?
- Did you need to ad-lib any of the words or phrases (this can actually be a positive)?
- Do you feel you appeared to be physically relaxed during the performance?

Try this as an exercise, just for your own information. The outcome will enable you ascertain where you need to focus your additional work, or allocate more time, in the future.

It's quite common for Chapter of Improvement to hold a little Post-Mortem at some point following a meeting. You should try to attend, because this is probably the only time you can expect to get something like an honest critique of your Work.

Filling the Gap in Your Life!

For many people, the next day after the meeting is a bit of an anti-climax. Because you spent the last few weeks working to a disciplined schedule, now that the pressure is off, you'll find gaps in your life with nothing to fill them.

Having established that you can follow the System, and fit learning around and inside your normal daily routine, it's important not to lose the structure. You've re-organised your life to accommodate Ritual Learning, so why would you want to go back to the old way of doing things?

If you are in a Working Office, such as PS, or maybe one of the Principal's Chairs, it's quite simple. You should already know what the Work is going to be at the next meeting, and what your part is going to entail, and if you don't, a quick e-mail or SMS to the Chapter Secretary will soon provide the answer. So you can go straight to the Book and start working on your next Ceremony. Hopefully there is enough time for you to set up the process as we did before.

Alternately, if you were delivering a Lecture 'out of office', it's really important not to wait until the next Standing Committee or Chapter of Improvement to get your assignment, because if that's a few days or weeks away, you'll be losing time and slipping out of the system you learned. So be smart; even if you don't know what work might be available to you at the next meeting, you should know what Ceremony is planned, so pick the most appropriate work, and start on it straight away. As we explained earlier, if you're an active attendee at Standing Committee or CoI, you can usually manoeuvre yourself into the position of being invited to do the work you want, at least some of the time.

Your Masonic career is long, so no Ritual will ever be wasted.

When it comes to the Lectures, utilise the recommended

timetable of each of the major Ceremonies, which is shown in Appendix A.

This time you are smarter than you were the first time. You will have figured out the techniques that worked really well for you. For example, do you need to allow more time for the first Stage, the 'cramming' of the work? Or maybe that was fine but it took longer than you thought to iron out the kinks in Stage Two. Whatever the case, you are the best person to judge your own capabilities. You can use whichever of the techniques worked for you, and indeed add to them if you found methods or variations that worked better.

But you must stick to the Three-Stage Approach; Cramming, Polishing and Rehearsing.

Remember: C.P.R.

Re-Learning and Revising

Once you've gone through the pain of learning something once, and delivered it, the second time is a lot easier, because if you learned it well enough to deliver it competently, then you have successfully implanted it into your subconscious memory, and it has become a part of you. So dragging it back to the surface a second time is going to be a lot easier than learning it all over again, and the third time will be easier still.

The first time I was required to perform the Mystical Lecture (the 'big one') from the Z Chair was during my year as First Principal. Using most of the methods previously explained, and with the assistance of an occasional Chapter of Improvement, it took me around four months to get it to the point where I was able to deliver it. I won't say that it was flawless: far from it. I am sure I made a lot of mistakes, many of which I managed to cover without anyone noticing, and I probably took a few prompts as well. But it went OK, we didn't kill or even injure the candidate, and we had a nice drink afterwards.

The next time I did the Ceremony was a few years later, and it took me a month and one CoI to get it done. The performance was infinitely better than the first time, though still not perfect.

Since then I have grabbed the opportunity to do the Lecture maybe six or seven times, and these days it takes around a fortnight of revision and one complete run through at CoI and it's done. It's still not perfect, I still miss a sentence out here and there, and occasionally I'll need a prompt (because I'm getting a bit older now), but these days I only need the Book, or rather the transcript on my Smartphone, to get it done.

So I made it one of my specialisations. Whenever there is an Exaltation imminent, I make sure that I have revised it just in case. Because you never know what might happen or when you might have to step up at the last minute and fill in for someone whose car wouldn't start!

These days, Grand Chapter encourages the 'splitting up' of the larger Ceremonies, so that more Companions can be involved, and this is a great strategy for Chapters. If your Chapter has adopted the Permitted Alternative Version of the Ritual, there are lots of opportunities for you to participate.

In my own case, I try to maintain the Mystical Lecture, which is compulsory at an Exaltation, and the PS Exaltation Ceremony and in a current condition all the time, so that I am able to step in and take on any individual part of it if needed, even at short notice. This is good for me, because it provides a regular opportunity to work in the Chapter, and it's good for the Chapter, because it gives them options. You might consider something similar yourself.

Recommended Timetable for Chapter Ceremonies

Ceremony	Days Required for Each Stage			
	Cram	Polish	Re-hearse	Total
P.S. Exaltation (complete)	60	30	30	120
J. Installing Successor	24	12	12	48
J. Robes & Sceptres	10	5	5	20
J. Historical Lecture	40	20	20	80
J. Exaltation (P.A.V.)	8	4	4	16
H. Installing Successor	30	15	15	60
H. Robes & Sceptres	12	6	6	24
H. Symbolical Lecture (Trad)	50	25	25	100
H. Symbolical Lecture (P.A.V.)	20	10	10	40
H. Exaltation (P.A.V.)	8	4	4	16
Z. Installing Successor	24	12	12	48
Z. Robes & Sceptres	10	5	5	20
Z. Mystical Lecture Pt1 (Trad)	40	20	20	80
Z. Mystical Lecture Pt2 (Trad)	40	20	20	80
Z. Mystical Lecture Pt1 (P.A.V.)	20	10	10	40
Z. Mystical Lecture Pt2 (P.A.V.)	20	10	10	40
Z. Mystical Lecture Pt3 (P.A.V.)	12	6	6	24
Z. Exaltation (Trad)	60	30	30	120
Z. Exaltation (P.A.V.)	60	30	30	120
Presentation of GC Cert.	30	15	15	60
Address to Companions	20	10	10	40

Conclusion

If you are serious about Ritual, either because you are working your way through the Offices in order to eventually take a Chair in your Chapter, or alternately if you are simply interested in participating in the Chapter by delivering Certificate presentations or the other Principal's Lectures, there is no reason why you should ever be in a position where you are not learning or preparing the next piece of work.

If you adopt this philosophy, you will always have something to occupy you in a quiet moment. And you will always have a way of getting to sleep at night!

Finally

If you have found this book useful and would like to receive updates or make any contribution to future editions, please register at **www.learningmasonicritual.com** and/or join the Facebook Page "Learning Masonic Ritual".

Thank you for buying the book and please Review it on Amazon if you like!

S&F

Rick Smith

Also by Rick Smith

HOW TO MASTER SELF HYPNOSIS IN A WEEKEND

The Simple, Systematic and Successful Way to **Get Everything You Want**

RICK SMITH
HPD, DHyp

Available in Paperback or Kindle E-Book

Printed in Great Britain
by Amazon